BAHRAIN

BAHRAIN

The Modernization
of Autocracy

Fred H. Lawson

Westview Press
BOULDER, SAN FRANCISCO, & LONDON

To the memory of
Malcolm H. Kerr
who taught me that studying
Arab politics could be fun

Westview Profiles/Nations of the Contemporary Middle East

Copyright © 1989 by Westview Press, Inc.

Published in 1989 in the United States of America by Westview Press, Inc., 5500 Central Avenue, Boulder, Colorado 80301, and in the United Kingdom by Westview Press, Inc., 13 Brunswick Centre, London WC1N 1AF, England

Library of Congress Cataloging-in-Publication Data
Lawson, Fred Haley, 1952–
  Bahrain: the modernization of autocracy/Fred H. Lawson.
    p. cm.—(Westview profiles. Nations of the contemporary Middle
East)
  Bibliography: p.
  Includes index.
  ISBN 0-8133-0123-8
  1. Bahrain. I. Title. II. Series
DS247.B2L39 1989
953′.65—dc19   88-28690
                                                                    CIP

Printed and bound in the United States of America

The paper used in this publication meets the requirements of the American National Standard for Permanence of Paper for Printed Library Materials Z39.48-1984.

10   9   8   7   6   5   4   3   2   1

Contents

Illustrations

Preface

Present-day Bahrain is at the same time unique among the Arab oil-producing Gulf states and indicative of future developments in these amirates. Its uniqueness lies in the social, political, and economic structures of the country: The indigenous population is characterized by a peculiar set of overlapping cleavages; the country's industrial work force has a history of militant action and a degree of political consciousness unmatched in neighboring states; and the islands' economy has achieved a level of diversification into non-petroleum-related activities that is the envy of planners in the surrounding area. But at the same time, Bahrain's rulers confront the same problems that face those of the other smaller Arab Gulf states: rapid urbanization, increasing numbers of immigrant laborers, dramatic fluctuations in the price of petroleum on international markets, and growing instability in the region as a whole. And because the country's oil reserves are relatively limited and are being rapidly depleted, the regime has considerably fewer resources to use in meeting these challenges than it had in previous decades. How Bahrain's dominant social coalition deals with this situation may well set a precedent for other oil-producers on the Arab side of the Gulf.

This study provides an overview of current trends on the islands and of the social and historical context from which they have emerged. It is intended as an introduction to Bahraini affairs for the general reader and thus makes use of the existing literature wherever possible. So as not to discourage the uninitiated, the use of Arabic terms in the text has been kept to a minimum, and only works in English are included in the Notes and Suggestions for Further Reading. The social basis for the country's political and economic affairs is laid out in Chapter 1. The history of the islands is outlined and the circumstances under which Great Britain took control of them during the latter half of the nineteenth century are reviewed in Chapter 2. The story of the rise and fall of the most important movements aimed at overthrowing the imperial regime is told in Chapter 3. Chapters 4 and 5 are sketches of the most significant features of Bahrain's contemporary political and economic systems. Finally, in Chapter 6, the country's foreign policy is discussed and the ways traced in which the government has tried to cope with a variety of external threats.

Although the book is not a detailed scholarly monograph, it does include some new interpretations of Bahraini affairs. This is partly because there remain serious gaps in the literature on the islands' history and politics and partly because works on more recent events often neglect crucial matters. Thus, I do not believe anyone else has told the story of the nationalist movements of the 1950s quite the way I have; no other study has put trends in the country's economy into the same categories I do; and I am sure no one else has attempted to present a Bahraini perspective on international relations in the Gulf. All of these interpretations will no doubt be viewed as controversial. But I trust they will stimulate further thinking and fieldwork about this pivotal and fascinating country.

David Long and Lawrence Shrader read successive drafts of this study in their entirety and provided me with meticulous criticisms, all of which improved the presentation and argumentation of the final product. Rosemarie Said Zahlan sent me a copy of the modern history proceedings of the Bahrain Through the Ages Conference convened by the Bahrain Historical and Archaeological Society in December 1983, along with much-appreciated words of encouragement at the start of the project. Karen Pfeifer made helpful suggestions concerning the organization of the chapter on contemporary economic trends, and John Voll checked my remarks on Islamic jurisprudence against his encyclopedic knowledge of the subject. By making an exception in my case, Ruth Baacke of the George Camp Keiser Library of the Middle East Institute made it possible for me to acquire copies of essential source materials; Laurie Brand not only played an accessory role in this particular caper but has also been an unfailing source of succor. Barbara Wimpee took time away from remodeling her house to prepare the map of the islands. Grants from the faculty development committees of Smith College and Mills College supported the initiation and completion of this study, respectively; whatever utility the resulting book may have as a teaching tool is a direct result of my association with these two exceptional institutions. At Smith, Carolyn Lattin ferreted out a number of vital references during the early stages of the project. At Mills, Trina Lieras and David Wells-Roland-Holst transformed confusing lists of statistical data into comprehensible tables, while Ruth Cohen produced the photographs. Finally, I owe considerable debts to Nancy Campagna, for the obsolescent typewriter, and to my wife, Deborah, for the hours I spent pounding away at it.

Fred H. Lawson
Oakland, California

Notes to the Reader

1. Transliteration of Arabic words and names has generally followed the system adopted by the *International Journal of Middle East Studies*, with the exception of commonly used place names, e.g., Manama. The symbol ' represents the Arabic consonant *'ayn*.

2. The Arabic definite article has been transliterated al- and attached to its referent; the homonym *Al* indicates the Arabic term for extended family or clan, as in the Al Khalifah.

3. The more or less neutral term *the Gulf* has been used throughout the text to refer to the Arab/Persian Gulf separating the Arabian peninsula from the coast of Iran.

F.H.L.

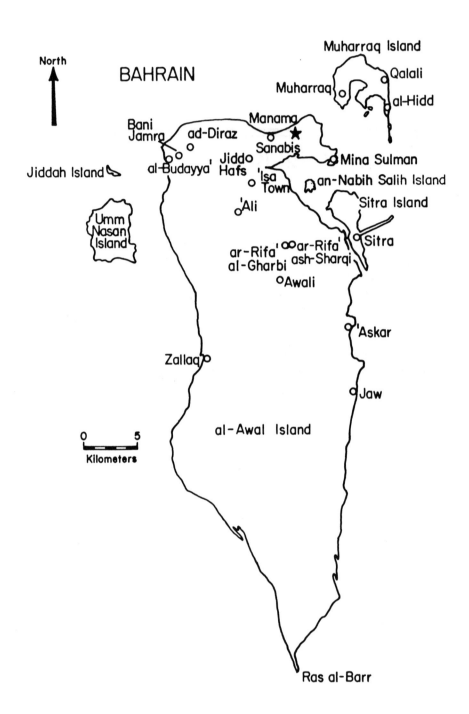

North

BAHRAIN

Muharraq Island

Qalali

Muharraq

al-Hidd

Bani
Jamra

ad-Diraz

Manama

Sanabis

Jiddah Island

al-Budayya'

Jiddo
Hafs

'Isa
Town

Mina Sulman

an-Nabih Salih Island

Sitra Island

Umm
Nasan
Island

'Ali

ar-Rifa'
al-Gharbi

ar-Rifa'
ash-Sharqi

Sitra

Awali

'Askar

Zallaq

Jaw

0   5

Kilometers

al-Awal Island

Ras al-Barr

1

Geographical and Social Structure

This chapter, covering Bahrain's geography and the important aspects of its social structure, its changing demographic trends, and its culture, sets the stage for the history and political and economic analysis that follow.

GEOGRAPHY

Dawlat al-Bahrain, the State of Bahrain, consists of 33 islands lying in the heart of the Gulf, approximately 24 kilometers (15 miles) off the northeast coast of Saudi Arabia and 21 kilometers (13 miles) to the northwest of the Qatar peninsula (see Map 1.1). Almost 85 percent of the country's total land area of some 650 square kilometers (250 square miles) is accounted for by the largest island in the archipelago, al-Awal (also known as Bahrain Island), which is about 16 kilometers (10 miles) wide at the northern end and tapers to a point at Ras al-Barr around 48 kilometers (30 miles) to the south. This island houses the capital city of Manama, almost all of the country's arable land, and the oil-producing area around Jabal ad-Dukhan. A causeway joins al-Awal to the adjacent island of Muharraq to the northeast—on which are located the country's second-largest city (Muharraq), the international airport, and the docks of the Arab Shipbuilding and Repair Yard (ASRY). A bridge leads from al-Awal to the island of Sitra along its eastern coast; Sitra contains the petroleum loading terminal and tank farm belonging to Bahrain Petroleum Company.

The much smaller island of an-Nabih Salih lies between al-Awal and Sitra and was in the past completely covered with date palms. Jiddah and Umm Nasan, just off the northwestern shore of the main island, are the only other notable components of the archipelago; these serve as the country's prison and as a private game preserve and garden

1

Map 1.1

for the ruler, respectively. The remaining islands in the group, with the exception of the more distant Hawar Islands just off the western coast of Qatar, are virtually uninhabitable.

Climatic conditions on the islands are for the most part severe; from June to September temperatures reach 48°C (120°F) and the humidity is often nearly 80 percent. During the winter months, temperatures range from 14° to 24°C (55° to 75°F), but the humidity often rises to more than 90 percent. The prevailing wind from December to March, called the Shamal, brings damp air over the archipelago from the southeast, along with occasional dust storms. Summers are buffeted by hot, dry Qaws winds from the southwest, but the hottest weeks in June may be relieved by a cooler Barra wind from the south during some years.

On those rare occasions when rain falls at all—the annual rainfall averages less than 10 centimeters (4 inches)—it tends to come in short bursts that flood the shallow dry creek beds (*wadis*) and hinder travel along the islands' unimproved secondary roads. Agriculture is thus dependent upon artesian springs, and the most favorable lands for cultivation make up less than 14 percent of the total land area, leaving the largest proportion of the archipelago barren.

STRUCTURE OF BAHRAINI SOCIETY

Although Bahrain is conventionally considered a "traditional" Arab society, in which social relations are primarily determined by tribal or religious factors, such a picture of the structure of local society is seriously misleading. The country differs substantially from both Saudi Arabia, where social interaction takes a form that more closely approximates that of purely tribal or lineage societies, and Qatar, where local society is at the same time more homogeneous in ethnic and religious terms and more clearly differentiated into dominant and subordinate classes. Bahraini society shares some of the features of the societies found in the surrounding amirates, but it is distinguished by the way in which cleavages based on ethnicity, class position, and national origin overlap to produce a matrix of social relations unique to the islands.

Sectarian Divisions

Perhaps the most obvious way of characterizing Bahraini society is in terms of ethnic or sectarian composition: Somewhere around one-third of the islands' 240,000 citizens follow the tenets of the majority Sunni branch of Islam, whereas the remaining two-thirds belong to the largest of the religion's Shi'i offshoots. The precise distribution of Sunnis and Shi'a among the country's population is open to question, as the last official census in which religious identification was reported was taken in 1941. At that time, Muslims made up 98 percent of the indigenous population, of which just under 53 percent were classified as Shi'is. According to the best available estimates, the proportion of Bahraini citizens belonging to the Shi'a approached 70 percent during the mid-1980s.[1] But such gross figures mask distinctions within each of these two communities that play a crucial role in structuring social and political relations in the country as a whole.

Despite their numerical disadvantage, Sunnis have formed the dominant religious community in Bahrain since at least the seventeenth century. Sunni predominance is buttressed by the fact that the country's most powerful social forces—notably the ruling Al Khalifah family, a majority of the most prominent merchant clans, and the Arab tribes allied to the Al Khalifah—all identify themselves with this branch of Islam. Since the last decades of the eighteenth century, when the Al

Khalifah migrated to the islands from Kuwait, religious authority has been closely tied to tribal authority; toward the end of the nineteenth century, the ruler appointed a single Sunni jurist to preside over court proceedings involving personal and family disputes among the various tribes residing on the islands.

Nevertheless, Bahrain's Sunni community is split into three distinct camps: one affiliated with the Maliki school of Islamic jurisprudence, another following the Hanbali tradition of legal interpretation, and a third that is predominantly Shafi'i in orientation. The Maliki camp includes the Al Khalifah and its tribal allies; adherents of this school of jurisprudence favor relatively strict interpretations of the tenets set down in the Quran and the traditions of the Prophet (Hadith), although they tolerate a degree of flexibility in applying the law under exceptional circumstances as long as the community as a whole benefits. The Hanbalis, on the other hand, are more prone to what Ignaz Goldziher calls "unquestioning belief in the literal meaning of the text" of the Quran and Hadith;[2] members of the country's commercial elite who trace their origins to the Arabian side of the Gulf make up the largest part of this camp. Finally, prominent merchant families whose progenitors immigrated to Bahrain from the Persian coast during the era in which the local pearl industry was prospering follow the system of interpretation associated with the Imam ash-Shafi'i, in which the principle of consensus is a crucial criterion for establishing the validity of legal judgments. This group is known collectively as the Hawala.

Shi'is on the islands are virtually all adherents of the Twelver form of Shi'i Islam, in which the twelfth and hidden Imam—Muhammad, the son of al-Imam Hasan al-'Askari—is revered as the once and future exemplar of religious piety. Furthermore, the Bahraini Shi'a share a long history of doctrinal and political convergence with the Shi'i populations of Iran and the pilgrimage cities of Najaf and Karbala in southern Iraq.[3] Within this widespread Shi'i community, the Usuli school of legal interpretation—which accepts the Quran, the Hadith, the consensus of the community, and the exercise of intellect as equivalent bases for the authoritative derivation of doctrine and law—predominates. But significant pockets of the less rationalistic Akhbari school—which asserts the primacy of received traditions associated with the Quran and the twelve successive Imams as the foundation for both doctrine and jurisprudence— survive on the islands, as they do in isolated areas of southern Iraq.

These divisions belie the simplistic notion that Bahrain consists of a dominant Sunni majority and a subordinate Shi'i minority, the former having firm connections with the Arabian mainland and the latter strongly drawn to co-religionists in Iran and southern Iraq. In fact, serious doctrinal differences have on occasion contributed to the outbreak of severe conflicts between the Al Khalifah and the largely Hanbali tribes of eastern and central Arabia, as well as to sharp disagreements between the established religious authorities on the northern side of the Gulf and those based on the islands. Thus, religious orientation plays a significant but not a determinant part in shaping Bahraini social and political affairs. In order to understand the way that religion relates to day-to-day politics, one must consider how religious factors interact with the class and national dynamics underlying local society.

Class Structure

From a class perspective, it is useful to differentiate among three categories of forces in Bahraini society: a dominant class consisting of the central branch of the Al Khalifah and the more prominent members of the commercial oligarchy; a class of retainers made up of the Arab tribes allied to the Al Khalifah, the staff of the country's central administration, and the smaller traders and shopkeepers in the larger cities and towns; and a subordinate class composed of urban and rural workers, artisans and craftspeople, fisherfolk, and subsistence farmers. Conflicts of interest among these three classes have determined not only the broad pattern of coalition formation among the country's most powerful social forces but also the incidence and impact of political revolt on the islands.

At the center of Bahrain's dominant coalition stands the Al Khalifah, whose senior shaikhs have governed the country since the 1780s. The most powerful branch of the ruling family is composed of the direct descendants of Shaikh 'Isa bin 'Ali, who ruled the islands from 1869 to 1923 (see Figure 1.1). The shaikhs of the Al Khalifah consolidated their control over local society by confiscating much of the agricultural land on the archipelago in the late eighteenth century and organizing it into estates managed by designated members of the ruling family for the benefit of the clan as a whole.[4] It appears that the ruler himself (known as the *shuyukh*, or pre-eminent shaikh) administered the most important of these estates—namely, those of Muharraq Island, Sanabis, and al-Hidd—as well as the urban districts of Manama and Muharraq. Close relatives of the shuyukh held the remaining estates, subject to the ruler's approval. In more recent times, members of the Al Khalifah have made considerable fortunes speculating on the commercial development of these lands, particularly as real estate became more profitable than date cultivation in the early decades of the twentieth century.

Bahrain's commercial oligarchy consists of a limited number of established rich merchant families with long-standing ties to the Al Khalifah. Throughout the eighteenth and nineteenth centuries, these

6

Figure 1.1
Genealogy of the Central Branches of the Al Khalifah

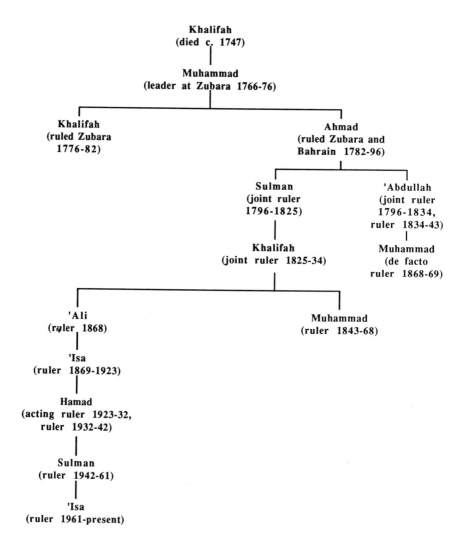

Source: Angela Clarke, *The Islands of Bahrain* (Manama: Bahrain Historical and Archaeological Society, 1981), p. 32.

families controlled the marketing of pearls harvested in the waters around the archipelago; they also served as moneylenders to the captains and divers who operated the pearling fleet, a role that gave them considerable power over the most profitable sector of the islands' economy in the pre-oil era.[5] With the beginnings of petroleum production and the expansion of the British presence in the country, the established rich merchant community turned to land speculation, construction, and the supplying of goods for use in the oilfield and the local naval and air bases as a way of surviving the collapse of the pearling industry. This community also acted as the country's primary bankers and money-changers, roles it has maintained to this day despite the government's policy of encouraging international financial concerns to set up regional offices on the islands. The most successful members of the commercial oligarchy defer to the Al Khalifah on most political and diplomatic issues, making them appear "deeply conservative" if not apolitical to outside observers.[6] But they remain a key component of Bahrain's dominant social coalition, providing not only financial support for the regime's industrial and commercial projects but also a source of expertise loyal to the ruling family in their roles as trusted personal advisers and administrators in the top layers of the central bureaucracy.

Closely tied to the country's dominant coalition are three groupings of retainers, forces that generally support the Al Khalifah and their rich merchant partners but have at their disposal substantially fewer resources than do the members of the ruling coalition. The first and oldest of these retainers are the Arab tribes allied to the Al Khalifah. These clans accompanied the ruling family to Bahrain in the late eighteenth century and share membership in the overarching Bani 'Utub confederation of north-central Arabia. Following the conquest of the islands, the more influential tribes, such as the Al Bin 'Ali and the Dawasir, were granted control over the pearling villages on the northern and eastern coasts of al-Awal. Despite the wealth generated by these villages, relations between the Al Khalifah and its allies have fluctuated dramatically over time: In the 1830s, rivalry between the ruling family and the Al Bin 'Ali flared into open warfare; in 1923, the Dawasir of al-Budayya' emigrated to Dammam on the coast of al-Hasa after a series of violent clashes with supporters of the economic and social reforms in the pearl industry proposed by the Al Khalifah and their British advisers.[7] Following the consolidation of Al Khalifah authority in the 1930s, the great majority of these tribespeople have adopted the role of subordinates to the ruler and his entourage and have been rewarded for their loyalty by appointment to second-level positions in the state bureaucracy and the armed forces.

A second group of retainers, the staff of the country's central administration, is more crucial to the affairs of modern-day Bahrain.

Top officials in the Bahraini government are drawn from the islands' established rich merchant community. But middle-level state employees are increasingly recruited from a wide range of groups in Bahraini society; and in the wake of the marked expansion of local education that began in the 1950s, positions in the central bureaucracy were consciously increased in an effort to coopt potential malcontents on the islands.[8] Many of these administrators make their homes in the newer state-supported housing projects in the suburbs of Manama, where rents are heavily subsidized and there are opportunities for home ownership.

Last of the regime's retainers are the smaller traders and shopkeepers who rely on the active or tacit cooperation of the commercial oligarchy for their own livelihoods. These petit bourgeois were hard-pressed to choose sides in the internecine rivalries that characterized elite politics on the islands during the late nineteenth and early twentieth centuries.[9] But with the consolidation of Al Khalifah predominance, they settled into a pattern of support for the status quo, as the status quo preserved a favorable orientation toward unrestricted private commercial activity. In more recent years, these traders have provided most if not all of the indigenous employees and managerial personnel for Bahrain's expanding financial and services enterprises.

Three diverse forces make up the subordinate class in contemporary Bahraini society. The first, and the one with the longest tradition of grievances against the dominant coalition, is composed of the country's indigenous agricultural workers and peasant cultivators. These laborers, who are predominantly Shi'i and make up the greatest proportion of the original inhabitants of the islands (called al-Baharnah), represented the mainstay of the country's domestic economy during the decades before 1900, although greater fortunes were made from controlling Bahrain's pearling fleet than from exploiting agricultural land. The precise history of the peasant communities on the islands remains obscure; nevertheless, the historical myth formulated by Shi'i villagers to account for their past illustrates a conception of harmonious order shared by peasants in other parts of the world. According to legend, Bahrain before the coming of the Al Khalifah consisted of 300 villages and 30 cities and towns, each ruled by a Shi'i jurist; these jurists were arranged in a hierarchy culminating in a three-person council whose status was confirmed by the entire population; property in general—and agricultural land in particular—was held on an individual basis according to the Islamic principle of *ihya'*, whereby the right of use accrues to whomever actually works the property. It is doubtful that the islands ever in fact operated on this basis, and no analogue to the political arrangement contained in this narrative has been found in any past or present Shi'i community.[10] Still, this story captures the agrarian and egalitarian ethos of Bahrain's rural laborers, while implicitly censuring the tribal structure of authority associated with the ruling family and its urban, rich merchant allies.

Although Bahrain's indigenous farmers appear to have suffered from the Al Khalifah's policy of confiscating the most productive agricultural land and turning it into commercial estates, the country's artisans and craftspeople in the more isolated villages were not subjected to the direct control of the ruling family and its tribal retainers. Communities such as Jidd Hafs, which was a center for the making of herbal medicines, Abu Saibi and Sanabis, which produced embroidered goods, and ad-Diraz and Bani Jamra, whose residents were renowned for their woven fabrics, retained a considerable degree of local autonomy clear up until the 1950s. These towns were generally larger than the surrounding agricultural villages in terms of both population and area and continue to this day to be characterized by extensive small-scale private land-holdings. Even more autonomous have been the isolated fishing villages lying along the eastern coast of al-Awal and Muharraq islands. The fishtraps used by the inhabitants of these communities, who are predominantly Shi'i, represented a form of small-scale private property that remained outside the purview of the regime as late as the 1960s, by which time a large proportion of these traps was held as endowments (*awqaf*) in the hands of the Shi'i Department of Awqaf located in Manama.[11]

More urban in character are the country's industrial workers and lower-level salaried employees. These proletarians are concentrated in the poorer districts of Manama and Muharraq, as well as in some of the older suburbs, such as al-Hidd. Their numbers include both Sunnis and Shi'a, and religious differences have on occasion served as a spark for intraclass conflict on the islands. On the whole, however, these workers stand in a similar position relative to the owners of Bahraini capital and tend to exhibit a level of class consciousness unmatched by wage laborers in the other Gulf amirates.[12] Indigenous workers have also tended to present a unified front in opposition to later immigrants, including not only the poorer ethnic Persians who arrived on the islands during the first decades of the twentieth century, but also the Omanis, Pakistanis, and Indians who came later.

National Origin

Bahraini society is structured not only on the basis of sectarian and class differences but also according to the area from which the members of different ethnic groups and classes emigrated to the islands. This third factor permeates social and political relationships at virtually all levels of local society but has its most significant impact on relations within the commercial oligarchy and the indigenous petite bourgeoisie.

On the whole, the country's urban mercantile elite consists of two components: one made up of families having their roots in central Arabia and another consisting of Sunni Arabs who immigrated to Bahrain from the Persian coast during the era in which the local pearl industry was prospering. The first of these broad groupings, whose members are generally referred to as Najdis, includes prominent families from the villages and towns of the Najd traditionally allied to the Al Khalifah but with close connections to other central Arabian clans now spread throughout the Gulf region. These contacts enabled the Najdis to develop an extensive trading and financial network along the southern shore of the Gulf; by expanding this family-based network to the Indian sub-continent, the Najdis played a key role as pearl suppliers to southern Asia as well. Although Sunni, these families are predominantly Hanbali rather than Maliki in orientation.

More numerous among the commercial oligarchy based in Manama are the established Persian-Arabs, or Hawala. These families also engaged in pearling during the late nineteenth and early twentieth centuries, although their members operated out of the city itself and did not take up residence in the outlying maritime villages dominated by the secondary tribes allied to the Al Khalifah. From their first decades on the islands, they have taken pains to emphasize their Arab heritage and play down their long association with Persian culture. Distinctions between the Hawala and other rich merchant houses had considerably greater political significance during the 1950s than they do at the present time.

Bahrain's indigenous smaller traders and shopkeepers include at least three distinct subgroupings in terms of national origin. The first consists of Sunnis hailing from Kuwait, many of whose ancestors accompanied the Al Khalifah to the islands in the late eighteenth century. The second is made up of Shi'i tradespeople with roots in al-Hasa. The third is the urban Persian Shi'a, whose members have faced long-standing antipathy from virtually all of the islands' other inhabitants.[13] This community is concentrated in two discrete districts of Manama, al-Hurra and al-Ajam, and represents the most segregated of the country's numerous minorities. Its members are excluded from membership in most of Bahrain's social and cultural clubs; consequently, they have been able to exert only minimal amounts of influence on the country's economic and political affairs. But their very isolation from the mainstream of Bahraini society has created a relatively high degree of corporate solidarity within this community. From the late 1920s to the early 1970s, the most important of the "mourning houses" (matam, to commemorate the martyrdom of al-Imam Husain in 680) organized by the Persian Shi'a of Manama was governed collectively by a council consisting of that community's most prominent merchants. Furthermore, the city's Persian population arranges processions to commemorate the martyrdom of the Imam Husain that are largely independent of those staged by the indigenous Shi'a.[14] In light of its fundamental marginality, this community could well provide the most receptive audience for the revolutionary appeals broadcast by more militant Shi'i clerics across the Gulf in Iran.

URBANIZATION AND INTERNAL MIGRATION

Bahraini society has been predominantly urban for most of the twentieth century. In the late 1950s almost 80 percent of the country's indigenous population lived in the larger cities and towns; at the time of the 1971 census this proportion had remained constant, with the great majority of city dwellers residing in the two largest cities, Manama and Muharraq, which together accounted for more than 70 percent of the country's inhabitants. The government estimates that the population of this combined metropolitan area grew by some 12 percent during the 1965–1971 period, a rate almost three times that of the growth of the local population as a whole. According to the 1981 census, rapid rates of growth have continued to characterize the larger cities and towns on the islands. Manama's population increased by more than one-third during the 1971–1981 period, while that of Muharraq grew by almost two-thirds. But the most dramatic increases occurred in the medium-sized towns just outside the metropolis: In the decade following the 1971 census, Jidd Hafs more than tripled in size, Sitra more than doubled, and the new 'Isa Town grew to include more than 21,000 inhabitants (see Table 1.1).

Manama and Muharraq represent centers of trade and transportation both for Bahrain itself and for the surrounding region. These two cities contain the great majority of the commercial and small-scale industrial establishments on the islands, as well as the primary government offices and foreign missions. The most important ports for goods coming into the country are Mina Sulman on the southern end of Manama and the older dhow harbor on the southwestern corner of Muharraq. The consolidation of power in the hands of the Al Khalifah and the commercial oligarchy based in the cities, along with the subsequent expansion of the central administration and the influx of foreign nationals that accompanied the rise of oil production, put these two cities in a position to dominate social and economic affairs on the islands during the twentieth century to a degree unprecedented in Bahrain's history.

As a result of these trends, Manama has become "a microcosm of Bahraini society, embodying the heterogeneous, cosmopolitan qualities

TABLE 1.1
Population of Bahrain's Urban Centers

	1959	1965	% Annual Increase	1971	% Annual Increase	1981	% Annual Increase
Manama	61,726	79,098	4.4	88,785	1.9	121,986	3.7
Muharraq	27,115	34,430	4.2	37,732	1.5	61,853	6.4
Jidd Hafs	5,591	7,941	6.3	11,152	5.8	33,693	20.2
ar-Rifa'	6,623	9,403	6.3	10,731	2.2	28,150	16.2
'Isa Town				7,501		21,275	18.4
Sitra	3,926	5,071	4.6	6,663	4.7	22,993	24.5
al-Hidd	4,440	5,230	2.9	5,269	0.1	7,111	3.5
Awali	3,123	2,097	-7.2	984	-13.4		
Total urban population	112,544	143,270	4.3	168,817	2.8	297,061	7.6
Total rural population	30,591	38,933	4.3	47,261	3.3	53,396	1.3
TOTAL	143,135	182,203	4.3	216,078	2.9	350,457	6.2

Source: Michael E. Bonine, "The Urbanization of the Persian Gulf Nations," in Alvin J. Cottrell, ed., *The Persian Gulf States* (Baltimore: Johns Hopkins University Press, 1980), p. 262; State of Bahrain, *Statistical Abstract 1982* (Manama: Central Statistics Organisation, August 1983), p. 5.

of the country" as a whole.[15] Sizeable populations of resident Persians, indigenous Arab Shi'a, native Arab Sunnis, Indians, Pakistanis, Baluchis, Omanis, and Yemenis, among many other smaller communities, live in this metropolitan area, for the most part without clustering into exclusive neighborhoods. Quarters with a distinctive character tend to be those that were swallowed up whole as Manama expanded during the 1960s and 1970s. Thus, al-Quful ("the returning") was formerly the site of a cistern filled by a number of springs, and Ras Rumman ("cape of pomegranate") used to be famous for its grove of pomegranate trees. At the same time, areas clearly associated with prominent merchant families continued to be known by the family name, such as Kanu along the northern shore and the neighboring district of Fariq al-Fadil.

Muharraq differs in two important respects from Manama. In the first place, the city has a considerably more homogeneous population; it consists primarily of indigenous Sunni Arabs having no clear ties to the more prominent tribal clans. Tribespeople allied to the Al Khalifah moved out of the city during the 1930s, when the pearl industry declined and the ruler transferred his official residence to the outskirts of Manama. Consequently, few newer groups moved into the city after the 1940s, and only the districts of Fariq al-Hayayish ("the weavers") and as-Sagha ("the goldsmiths"), both populated by indigenous Shi'i Arabs, deviated from the city's virtually uniform Sunni Arab composition. Second, Muharraq has attracted substantially smaller amounts of investment capital than has Manama, leaving it with a population consisting primarily of lower-income salaried workers. This trend has left the residents of the city with fewer of the private and public resources necessary to keep up with the inhabitants of the more affluent districts in and around Manama; thus, the population of Muharraq is particularly susceptible to mobilization for political action. As Fuad Khuri remarks, "with this social and ethnic composition, Muharraq has been a bastion for pan-Arab, pan-Islamic movements; organized protests and rebellions against national and international policies have always found a respectable following in this city."[16]

Boundaries among Bahrain's urban, village, and rural districts have tended to become blurred by the substantial linkages that bind these diverse communities together. The combination of short distances, improvements in transportation and communication, and an integrated marketing system has transformed the country into what Khuri calls a "metrocommunity" that combines a metropolis—the two larger cities—with a series of smaller suburban "villages."

Villages having histories as agricultural centers lie mostly in a semicircular area along the northern and northwestern coast of al-Awal. The residents of these villages have significantly lower literacy rates than do the inhabitants of other parts of the country and speak a distinctive dialect of Arabic that sets them apart as rustic and uncultured to the ears of their urban neighbors. Several of these communities have in recent years become virtual suburbs of Manama, from which skilled and unskilled workers commute to salaried jobs in the metropolis each day. Jidd Hafs, Sulmaniyyah, al-Quful, and Sanabis, for example, are practically indistinguishable in social terms from Shi'i districts of the city itself. A notable exception to this pattern is the village of al-Budayya', whose Sunni inhabitants took over the area when most of the Dawasir tribe emigrated to al-Hasa and where the government has set up an agricultural research station to promote improved farming techniques.

Villages with histories as fishing and pearling centers include al-Budayya' and Zallaq on the western coast of al-Awal, 'Askar and Jaw on the eastern coast of al-Awal, and Qalali and al-Hidd on the eastern tip of Muharraq island. Most of the residents of these villages who remained following the collapse of the pearl industry on the islands have gradually joined the residents of the agricultural villages in commuting to the metropolis to work. But fishing has not disappeared entirely from these communities; privately owned fishtraps still dot the coastline off several of these villages. The population of al-Hidd in particular continued to grow throughout the early 1960s, albeit at a much more moderate rate than that of Bahrain's other urban areas. By the early 1980s, however, al-Hidd had been overtaken by the spectacular growth that characterized the towns to the west and south of the metropolis (see Table 1.1).

Bahrain's arid interior includes three distinct kinds of communities. The first, of which the sister towns of ar-Rifa' al-Gharbi and ar-Rifa' ash-Sharqi are the sole examples, is made up of essentially bedouin settlements. These settlements were established during the mid-nineteenth century as redoubts for the Al Khalifah and its closest allies. They have immediate access to the best springs and grazing lands on al-Awal and have traditionally enjoyed a reputation for clean, healthy air. In 1952 Shaikh Sulman moved his official residence to ar-Rifa' al-Gharbi, prompting several other prominent members of the country's tribal and commercial elite to build residences nearby. By the mid-1970s, a new palace for the ruler and an audience chamber for the crown prince had been constructed in the town. These institutions have effectively transferred the center of current political affairs on the islands from Manama to ar-Rifa' and its environs. Both the newly established Arab Gulf University and the country's police training college lie within hailing distance of these twin towns.

'Ali represents an entirely different sort of interior community. This village is home for two industrial activities that long predate the production of petroleum on the islands: the production of clay pottery and the manufacture of lime. The pottery industry involves the shaping and firing of handmade waterpipes, incense burners, and ornamental flower pots; most of these items are exported to the eastern province of Saudi Arabia. Small numbers of clay ovens used for baking bread in nearby districts are also produced in the village. These operations are carried out by a single family firm using local labor. Lime manufacturing involves the firing, cracking, and pulverizing of stone quarried on the islands, utilizing kilns located in ancient burial mounds on the edge of the village. This product is also primarily exported to Saudi Arabia, although small amounts of prepared lime are also used in Bahrain's construction industry as a whitewashing compound.

Finally, the oil settlement of Awali, lying just north of Jabal ad-Dukhan, has provided the prototype for the series of planned communities that have been built on the islands over the last fifty years. This town was constructed from scratch during the mid-1930s, as the number of employees at the oilfield grew too large to be housed at the company's original camp. By the end of the decade it consisted of a dozen dormitories, each surrounded by porches and walls to deflect the sun and wind and each connected to what must have been the first multiunit central air-conditioning system in the world. In 1959 the town had a population of more than 3,000, making it almost as large as the much better established villages of al-Hidd and Sitra. But during the 1960s, the number of residents at Awali dropped precipitously, leaving fewer than 1,000 permanent inhabitants at the site by the mid-1970s. As production operations at the Jabal ad-Dukhan field continue to decline, Bahraini oil workers find it more convenient to live at the newer planned communities being constructed by the government on the outskirts of Manama.

At least two significant problems have arisen for the Bahraini authorities as a result of the growing concentration of the country's population in a limited number of heavily urbanized areas. First, the drain on the islands' once-substantial water supply has become increasingly severe over the last 20 years or so. In the 5 years after 1968, water consumption rose from just under 4 million gallons (15 million liters) per day to 5.5 million gallons (21 million liters) per day. By 1978, this figure had jumped to more than 18 million gallons (68 million liters) per day, and in 1982 the government reported that more than 30.4 million gallons (115 million liters) of fresh water were being consumed each day in the country.[17] Continued increases in water use threaten to outrun the capacity of both the existing groundwater supply network and the state-owned desalination plant at Sitra.

Artisan firing lime in a kiln constructed within one of the ancient burial mounds outside 'Ali. Source: Michael Jenner, *Bahrain: Gulf Heritage in Transition* (London: Longman, 1984), p. 67.

In the spring of 1982, state officials responded to the growing water supply crisis by contracting with a Swedish consulting firm to prepare a comprehensive plan to meet the rising demand for fresh water. The final draft of this plan called for the construction of a system of new desalination plants with a combined capacity of 25 million gallons (95 million liters) per day. To oversee the implementation of this plan, a new committee for water resources was created in May of that year, consisting of five cabinet ministers and the head of the municipality of Manama under the direction of the prime minister, Shaikh Khalifah bin Sulman. The Italian construction company Italimpianti began work on three large-scale desalination plants on Sitra island during the summer of 1982; at the same time, the committee for water resources ordered a number of pumping stations connected to artesian wells outside the capital shut down and installed meters to regulate daily outflow on the remainder. These measures have helped alleviate the problem, although water shortages continue to occur on the islands during the summer months when water consumption is at its peak. In November 1985 a British bottling company agreed to supply almost 16,000 2-liter (2.1-quart) bottles of spring water a week to a local chain of supermarkets; the contract was reportedly worth $2.1 million per year.

Second, the shortage of dwellings in urban districts has driven the cost of living up sharply, increasing the demand for government subsidies not only for housing but for other necessities as well. During the 30 years after 1941, the number of houses available on the islands increased by an average of about 2.6 percent per year, while the indigenous population grew at a rate of around 3 percent per year. The shortfall in housing has been particularly marked in the larger urban areas: Government figures show that the number of houses in Manama rose by around 6.7 percent per year from 1941 to 1971, as the indigenous population of the city increased by almost 7.3 percent per year. This trend has led to a rapid deterioration in the quality of available housing as well as to substantial overcrowding in existing units. The Ministry of Housing estimated in 1976 that nearly 72 percent of the dwellings in the country stood in need of major repairs or renovation and that the mean occupancy ratio for the islands was 2.6 persons per room.[18] Moreover, the lack of available housing has generated agglomerations of substandard shanties, called *barastis*, at the margins of Manama and its suburbs, although the extent of these "spontaneous settlements" has been steadily reduced since the early 1960s as a result of the government's active support for the construction of low-income residences. Unfortunately, a sizeable proportion of the new housing on the islands has been built on land having a high degree of salinity, sharply reducing

Modern housing units in 'Isa Town. Source: Michael Jenner, *Bahrain: Gulf Heritage in Transition* (London: Longman, 1984), p. 90.

(because of corrosion of the metal and cement structures) the expected lifetime of these newer buildings.

IMMIGRANT AND EXPATRIATE WORKERS

In addition to the indigenous population, Bahrain attracts substantial numbers of foreign workers, on both short-term and long-term bases. According to the 1965 census, non-Bahrainis made up just over 21 percent of the country's total population; by 1971 this proportion had dropped to 17.5 percent; in 1976 it had again risen to just under 24 percent. The 1981 census indicates that both the number and the percentage of foreign nationals on the islands has risen markedly since the mid-1970s. Non-Bahrainis now constitute almost 32 percent of the total population, or approximately 112,400 persons. This means that in spite of the government's effort to restrict immigration during the late 1970s, more foreign workers were present in the country in 1981 than the World Bank had projected for 1985, even with assumptions that turned out to be overly optimistic.[19]

J. S. Birks and C. A. Sinclair show that expatriates play a key role in Bahrain's economy. More than one-third of the total labor force was composed of nonnationals at the time of the 1971 census; by mid-decade almost 40 percent of a substantially expanded work force was made up

TABLE 1.2
Composition of Bahraini Work Force by Sector and Nationality
(percents)

	1971		1981	
	Bahraini	Non-Bahraini	Bahraini	Non-Bahraini
Agriculture & fishing	75.1	24.9	49.7	50.3
Mining	95.3	4.7		
Manufacturing	66.0	34.0	45.3	54.7
Electricity	86.8	13.2	11.2	88.8
Construction	54.2	45.8	7.5	92.5
Trade	63.0	37.0	10.5	89.5
Transportation	65.4	34.6	52.3	47.7
Finance	68.3	31.7	62.3	37.7
Services	59.4	40.6	7.1	92.9
Not adequately described	77.6	22.4		

Source: Economic Commission for Western Asia, *Statistical Abstract of the Region of the Economic Commission for Western Asia 1968-1976* (Beirut: ECWA, 1978), p. 5; State of Bahrain, *Statistical Abstract 1982* (Manama: Central Statistics Organisation, August 1983), p. 266.

of non-Bahrainis.[20] Figures reported by the 1981 census indicate a startling increase in the number of economically active foreign workers on the islands: In mid-1977 the total number of employed expatriates stood at 39,700; four years later it had jumped to 80,700. In 1982 alone the authorities issued 26,562 labor permits to expatriates, with the largest proportion going to craftspeople and industrial workers, services personnel, and professional and technical workers, in that order. Non-Bahrainis accounted for almost 55 percent of the country's manufacturing employees, more than 92 percent of the construction workers, and around 93 percent of those employed in services that year (see Table 1.2).

As the total number of immigrant workers on the islands rose beginning in the mid-1970s, the composition of the expatriate work force underwent significant change as well. In 1971 South Asians accounted for almost one-third of the total number of migrant laborers coming into the country and more than one-quarter of all employed foreigners; by 1977, immigrants from India, Pakistan, and other Asian countries represented more than two-thirds of the expatriate workers entering Bahrain and just under two-thirds of immigrants with jobs. These workers largely displaced immigrants from other Arab countries, particularly those from Oman, and from Iran; moderate increases in the number of workers coming from Iraq and other parts of the Gulf, as well as slightly greater numbers of Egyptians entering the country, failed to offset the large-scale exodus of Omanis from the islands that took place during the late 1970s. By 1981, growing numbers of Korean, Thai, and Filipino laborers were arriving in the country, further accentuating the shift away from Arab expatriates and toward South and East Asian workers. Britons and Americans also appear to have been entering Bahrain in increasing numbers in the 1980s.

Most expatriates find employment in the private sector of the Bahraini economy, particularly in manufacturing, construction, and services. But as the public sector has expanded during the last decade or so, foreign nationals have come to occupy increasing numbers of managerial and technical positions in state-affiliated concerns as well. Thus, the 3,900 non-Bahrainis employed in the public sector in 1971 represented approximately 27 percent of all government employees, whereas the 13,100 expatriates working in state enterprises ten years later made up 38 percent of the total. At the same time, however, the number of immigrants employed by Bahrain's most important state-sponsored enterprises fell during the early 1980s. Non-Bahrainis made up just under half of the employees at Bahrain National Oil Company in 1979 but less than a third of this company's labor force in 1982. Somewhat higher proportions of nonnationals were employed at Bahrain National Gas Company and the Gulf Petrochemicals Industry Company in 1982, but even in these concerns there are clear signs of a trend toward replacing foreign workers with indigenous personnel. So although it may indeed be the case that "'Bahrainization,' in any absolute sense, is simply out of the question,"[21] expatriates remain systematically excluded from those arenas most closely associated with the state, with the notable exception of foreign experts hired to advise the central administration itself.

Thus, although Bahrain resembles the other Gulf oil-producing states in having a significant and growing number of immigrant workers among its population, the country is distinguished by the relatively smaller proportion of the total labor force made up of foreign nationals. Moreover, the expatriate community on the islands is sharply bifurcated. On the one hand, this community includes an exceptionally high percentage of individuals with advanced degrees or specialized technical training. According to the 1981 census, almost one-third of non-Bahrainis in the general population had been educated at the secondary level or above, and almost 10 percent possessed a college or postgraduate degree. On the other hand, unskilled South and East Asian laborers are for the most part illiterate, segregated into substandard labor camps adjacent to the construction or industrial sites at which they work and paid minimal wages by the contractors who recruit them to the islands. The growing class of imported domestic servants, drawn largely from Sri Lanka and the Philippines, fares somewhat better but shares the underlying marginality common to all expatriates working in the amirate.

TRENDS IN THE ROLE OF WOMEN AND FAMILY LIFE

While Bahrain's total labor force more than tripled in size during the years from 1959 to 1981, the number of indigenous women working outside the home jumped 86 percent between 1965 and 1971 and another 560 percent from 1971 to 1981. This trend left Bahraini women participating in the work force at a higher rate than were women in any other Gulf state by the early 1980s. For the most part, work outside the home for these women is concentrated during the years between graduation from secondary school and marriage, or from the ages of 20 to 24. And it appears to be most closely associated with higher levels of education: Illiterate females have the lowest rates of participation in the labor force, whereas those who complete programs at the secondary level or beyond have dramatically higher rates of participation.[22]

Bahraini women employed outside the home tend to cluster in a limited number of occupations. Just over one-third of the country's working women hold professional or technical positions, particularly in the areas of teaching and nursing. Another third are employed in the services sector, particularly in social services. And about 30 percent of the indigenous female work force hold clerical positions of various kinds. To some extent these occupations have become earmarked for women in recent years, and Bahraini men tend to avoid entering them.

Although the trend toward greater female participation in the labor force should not be exaggerated—the 1981 census reports that just over 82 percent of Bahraini women do not work outside the home—this trend has generated a variety of significant changes in family patterns and relations between men and women on the islands. In the first place, a higher incidence of women working outside the home has accompanied a marked decline in the fertility rate on the islands. During the late 1960s, this rate averaged 208 births per thousand women; in the late 1970s, it had dropped to 145 per thousand. Second, marriage patterns, at least among the elite, have become increasingly restrictive. Khuri reports a noticeable decrease in the frequency of young women from the Al Khalifah marrying outside their primary descent group and a concomitant rise in the incidence of monogamy within the ruling family.[23] Third, Shirley Taylor observes that the long-standing custom of demanding a bride-price has begun to erode in the case of educated, and therefore employable, young women and that the tradition of family-arranged marriages is gradually giving way to arrangements negotiated between the prospective partners themselves.[24]

To what extent these shifts can be considered consequences of the expansion of educational opportunities for Bahraini women over the last two decades and how much they represent instead a disguised function of the greater latitude available to women associated with the islands' elite families is difficult to determine. As Khuri remarks, it is the more prominent Sunni households that have "the highest percentage of educated and employed women."[25] Furthermore, the ability to spend time working outside the home appears to be largely determined by the household's capacity to hire and retain domestic servants to take care of everyday chores. This option is not available to all households on the islands, although it may be spreading beyond the small group of elite families that formed the apex of Bahraini society during the first half of the twentieth century. The combination of government subsidies for the purchase of houses in the outlying development towns and flexible hours offered by some employers—notably, the islands' larger banking offices—has enabled women from even moderate-income families to follow in the footsteps of those from the more prominent families who opened up opportunities for female employment outside the home during the late 1960s.

CULTURAL DEVELOPMENTS

Contemporary Bahrain boasts a prominent and well-established artistic community that counts among its members a number of the most respected writers in the Gulf. These authors represent, on the one hand, the culmination of a long tradition of Arab poetry common to the region as a whole: Ibrahim al-'Urayyid and Ahmad Muhammad Al Khalifah compose lyrical reflections on romance and natural beauty in the refined style of classical Arab verse. But other, somewhat younger writers have elaborated new forms of poetic composition as a means of expressing the tensions facing Bahraini society in the modern age; for these poets, the impact of Western industrialism on Gulf society has entailed not only local nationalism and an expansion of individual opportunities but also a greater potential for exploitation and alienation. As a result, the newer generation of Bahraini authors tends to adopt a more committed tone and take as its themes such principles as social justice and freedom.

Perhaps the most famous of Bahrain's contemporary poets is Qasim Haddad. He was born on the islands in 1948 and developed a modernist style after dropping out of secondary school in the early 1960s. His reputation as both a poet and a proponent of intellectual and social change led to his appointment as director of culture and art at the Ministry of Information in 1983, as well as to his election as head of the Union of Bahraini Writers the following year. Among his better known collections of poetry are *The Good Omen* (1970), *Doomsday* (1980), and *Shrapnel* (1983). Similar in orientation is 'Ali 'Abdullah Khalifah, who was born in Bahrain in 1944. After serving as head of the Union of Bahraini Writers for three years during the early 1970s, he went on to set up a publishing house and a literary journal in an effort to provide outlets for experimental poetry and fiction for local authors. His own books include *The Moaning of the Masts* (1969) and *Illuminating the Memory of the Motherland* (1977).

Different in style, but equally concerned with political and social issues, is the verse of Hamdah Khamis. Born in 1946, she attended the University of Baghdad, where she took a degree in political science at the age of 22. After teaching for several years, Khamis became a columnist at the journal *al-Azminah al-'Arabiyyah* in the United Arab Emirates; she moved to *al-Fajr*, one of the Emirates' daily newspapers, in 1980. Her poetry is collected in *An Apology for Childhood* (1978). More complex and unconventional is the work of 'Ali ash-Sharqawi, who was born in Manama in 1948. He composes intricate but evocative verse while working as a veterinarian in the capital; his collected works include *Thunder in the Season of Draught* (1975) and *Psalm 23 for the Singer's Nectar* (1985). Ash-Sharqawi is the current head of the Union of Bahraini Writers.

CONCLUSION

Western stereotypes of Arab society bear little resemblance to life in contemporary Bahrain. The country's population is predominantly urban and is characterized by a class structure shaped by the islands' long history as an agricultural and commercial center. The inhabitants of the archipelago come from diverse areas, both from within and outside the Gulf, and practice a variety of different forms of Islam. Only in the more remote Shi'i villages and isolated quarters of Muharraq do women veil themselves from outsiders; in Manama and its suburbs, younger Bahraini women increasingly work outside the home, at least until they marry and have children. Literature and music have adapted to a wide range of newer styles and express the disorientation and difficulties of living in the industrial age, as well as an unromanticized nostalgia for the region's rapidly disappearing past. These trends make Bahrain one of the more complex societies of the Arab world and give it a distinct identity among the smaller Gulf states.

NOTES

1. Fahim I. Qubain, "Social Classes and Tensions in Bahrain," *Middle East Journal* 9(Summer 1955), p. 270; James A. Bill, "Islam, Politics, and Shi'ism in the Gulf," *Middle East Insight* 3(July-August 1984), p. 6.

2. Ignaz Goldziher, *Introduction to Islamic Theology and Law* (Princeton: Princeton University Press, 1981), p. 92.

3. Moojan Momen, *An Introduction to Shi'i Islam* (Oxford: George Ronald, 1985), Chapter 6.

4. Fuad I. Khuri, *Tribe and State in Bahrain* (Chicago: University of Chicago Press, 1980), Chapter 3.

5. See Muhammad Rumaihi, *Beyond Oil: Unity and Development in the Gulf* (London: Al Saqi Books, 1986), Chapter 1.

6. Michael Field, *The Merchants: The Big Business Families of Saudi Arabia and the Gulf States* (Woodstock, N.Y.: Overlook Press, 1984), p. 90.

7. Peter Lienhardt, "The Authority of the Shaykhs in the Gulf: An Essay in Nineteenth-Century History," in R. B. Serjeant and R. L. Bidwell, eds., *Arabian Studies*, vol. 2 (London: C. Hurst, 1975), pp. 66–67; Khuri, *Tribe and State*, pp. 94–99.

8. James H. D. Belgrave, "The Changing Social Scene in Bahrain," *Middle East Forum* 38(Summer 1962), pp. 62–66.

9. Khuri, *Tribe and State*, p. 96.

10. Ibid., pp. 28–29; R. B. Serjeant, "Fisher-folk and Fish-traps in al-Bahrain," *Bulletin of the School of Oriental and African Studies* 31(1968), p. 488.

11. Serjeant, "Fisher-folk and Fish-traps," pp. 506–507.

12. John Duke Anthony, *Arab States of the Lower Gulf: People, Politics, Petroleum* (Washington, D.C.: Middle East Institute, 1975), p. 61.

13. B. D. Hakken, "Sunni-Shia Discord in Eastern Arabia," *The Moslem World* 23(July 1933), pp. 302–305.

14. Khuri, *Tribe and State*, pp. 160, 167–168.

15. Ibid., p. 240.

16. Ibid., p. 253.

17. N. C. Grill, *Urbanisation in the Arabian Peninsula*, Centre for Middle Eastern and Islamic Studies, University of Durham, Occasional Papers Series, No. 25(1984), p. 66; State of Bahrain, Central Statistics Organisation, *Statistical Abstract 1982* (Manama, August 1983), Table 142.

18. Ibid., pp. 71–72, 74.

19. Rob Franklin, "Migrant Labor and the Politics of Development in Bahrain," *MERIP Reports* 132(May 1985), p. 9.

20. J. S. Birks and C. A. Sinclair, *Arab Manpower* (New York: St. Martin's, 1980), p. 169.

21. Franklin, "Migrant Labor," p. 11.

22. E. James Fordyce, Layla Rhadi, Maurice D. Van Arsdol, Jr., and Mary Beard Deming, "The Changing Roles of Arab Women in Bahrain," in Jeffrey B.

Nugent and Theodore H. Thomas, eds., *Bahrain and the Gulf* (New York: St. Martin's, 1985), p. 60.

23. Khuri, *Tribe and State*, p. 238.

24. Shirley B. Taylor, "Some Aspects of Social Change and Modernization in Bahrain," in Nugent and Thomas, eds., *Bahrain*, p. 50.

25. Khuri, *Tribe and State*, p. 238.

2

The Establishment of
the British Imperial Order

Bahrain's inhabitants have had a long and turbulent history. Its broad outlines consist of recurrent eras of commercial prosperity and intervening periods of warfare and foreign occupation. Prior to the nineteenth century, the islands served as a main base for a succession of local dynasties whose fortunes were derived from long-distance trade, augmented by profits from the indigenous pearling industry. With the ascendency of Great Britain in the Gulf beginning in the early 1800s, the cyclical pattern of regional politics was broken, and a more linear dynamic began to take shape, one in which the workings of British imperialism served to reinforce the predominance of the Al Khalifah within Bahraini society. Although the islands were never made a formal colony of the British empire, by the end of the nineteenth century they had been firmly integrated into an overarching imperial order centered on the British government in India. The incorporation of the archipelago into this imperial order enabled successive shuyukhs to distance themselves from neighboring rulers and consolidate their hold over political and economic affairs within this newly demarcated domain.

WAR AND TRADE IN
PRE-NINETEENTH-CENTURY BAHRAIN

Bahrain's rulers represented a dominant force in the commerce and diplomacy of the Gulf as early as the third millennium B.C., when their capital near the present site of Manama served as a central transshipment point in the extensive copper trade between Oman and Babylonia.[1] This culture appears to have reached the height of its economic prosperity and military power around 2000 B.C.; after that date the rise of Cyprus as a primary supplier of copper to Mesopotamia shifted the main arteries of long-distance trade in the Near East to the west.[2] When Alexander

the Great's armies passed through the region in the fourth century B.C.,
the primary occupations of the archipelago's residents were pearl fishing
and agriculture, although the islanders retained a reputation for commercial prowess well into the Roman era.[3]

By the time of the Prophet Muhammad, most of the eastern coast
of the Arabian peninsula was a tributary of the Sassanid empire in
Persia. But during the late sixth and early seventh centuries A.D., Bahrain
appears to have been subjected to domination by a variety of vassals
and opponents of this empire.[4] Even after al-'Ala bin al-Hadrami succeeded in adding the territory to the domain of Islam just after 632, a
succession of revolts kept affairs on the Gulf littoral unstable throughout
the next 700 years.[5] Al-Awal fell under the control of the maritime
empire of Hormuz during the early fourteenth century; around 1345 the
Hormuzi ruler Turanshah visited Manama, where the empire had built
its westernmost fort to protect the pearling operations whose product
made up a major part of its trade with India.[6]

As the Hormuzi empire declined in the late fifteenth century, a
bedouin dynasty named after its founder, Saif bin Zamil bin Jabr, took
over al-Awal and maintained high levels of order and prosperity on the
islands; in 1521 the Jabrid leader Muqrin tried unsuccessfully to construct
a battle fleet to resist the Hormuzis and their new allies, the Portuguese,
but a combined Hormuzi-Portuguese expeditionary force succeeded in
occupying Manama before the fleet could become operational. Bahrain
constituted a locus for periodic revolts against Portuguese domination
of the Gulf and for Ottoman-Portuguese rivalry for the next 80 years.
During this time, al-Awal's position as "a 'buffer' island separating the
rival powers and their limits of influence" enhanced both the diplomatic
importance of its rulers in regional affairs and its attractiveness as a
safe haven for merchants in the area.[7] According to a contemporaneous
account, it was the Portuguese-appointed governor's confiscation of the
property belonging to a wealthy pearl merchant that led to the ouster
of the Hormuzi-Portuguese garrison on the islands and their annexation
by the Persian Shah 'Abbas I.[8]

Bahrain remained subject to Persian rule from 1602 until 1782,
although Arab governors appointed by the shah generally supervised
day-to-day affairs on the islands. During this period, trade between
India and Iran flourished, and the British factory at Bandar 'Abbas
gradually achieved a dominant position in regional commerce. Continual
conflicts among rival factions on the northern Gulf littoral led officials
in the Bombay offices of the British East India Company to consider
relocating their local operations to Bahrain in the years around 1750.
The plan was abandoned when London decided that it would be too
difficult and costly to subdue the Hawala Arabs who dominated the

islands. When the East India Company's factory at Bandar 'Abbas was finally closed in March 1763, the British authorities moved their head-quarters, not to any of the port cities along the southern shore of the Gulf, but to Bushire, on the Persian coast, where trade could be carried on free from the depredations of "powerful Arab tribesmen."[9]

As British trade in the Gulf dropped off during the third quarter of the eighteenth century, local merchant houses captured a greater share of both regional and long-distance commerce. Prominent among these indigenous clans were the tribes that made up the Bani 'Utub, whose members had established themselves at Kuwait in the years after 1710. Under the rule of the Al Sabah, Kuwait became a primary entrepôt for trade between India and Syria during the middle years of the century. It also served as a base for pearling vessels that fished the waters around Bahrain under the auspices of two other clans of the 'Utub: the Al Khalifah and the Al Jalahima. When the former pulled out of Kuwait sometime around 1760, its members attempted to take up residence on the islands but were forced to move on by the Bani Madhkur, an Omani tribe whose chief ruled the archipelago on behalf of the shah of Persia and the Arab shaikh of Bushire. The Al Khalifah and their allies consequently settled at Zubara on the northwestern coast of the Qatar peninsula, whence they acquired a key role in the sea and land trade between Bahrain, on the one hand, and Qatar and al-Hasa, on the other, through a policy of levying no customs duties on goods passing through the port.[10]

By the 1780s, rivalry between the Bani 'Utub in Zubara and Kuwait and the rulers of other Gulf ports had grown intense. As a way of weakening the hold of the Al Khalifah on regional trade, the Bani Madhkur launched a series of raids on Zubara and its dependencies, prompting the Bani 'Utub to seize a number of ships belonging to merchants of Bushire and Bandar Riq and hold them for ransom. These actions led the shaikh of Bushire to send an expedition of 2,000 troops against Zubara in 1782, but this force was soundly defeated by the Al Khalifah while it was attempting to disembark outside the town. When a Kuwaiti fleet sailing to reinforce the Al Khalifah learned of the defeat, it changed course for Bahrain and captured the fort at Manama. The Al Khalifah and their allies immediately crossed the channel and took charge of mopping up the remainder of the Persian garrison. In the first months of 1783, Shaikh Ahmad bin Khalifah—surnamed "the Conqueror" by his followers—became the first ruler of Zubara and Bahrain, although he continued to reside at Zubara until his death in 1796.

By capturing Bahrain, the Al Khalifah substantially improved their position relative to those of other actors in the region. The rich merchants of Zubara already controlled a major portion of India's trade with the

Gulf. They were now joined by the pearl merchants of Manama and Muharraq, whose activities were estimated by the British to bring in almost 500,000 rupees annually—a figure 25 percent greater than the total value of the goods shipped each year to India from the ports on the Persian side of the Gulf. Soon after the occupation of Bahrain, merchants associated with the Al Khalifah acquired a fleet of ocean-going vessels constructed in India and began to carry cloth and metals from Surat directly to Kuwait and Basra for shipment on to Baghdad and Aleppo. In return, these merchants sent grain, dates, pearls, copper, saffron, and spices to the subcontinent. These operations severely undercut the reexport trade of Muscat, reducing that city's role to a subsidiary one of supplying coffee and spices from southern Arabia to the expanding commercial network centered on Bahrain and Zubara.

The growing prosperity of the cities dominated by the Al Khalifah made them attractive targets for both the ruler of Muscat and the Al Saud based in the Najd. The ruler of Muscat was prevented from moving against the islands by a struggle for succession to the sultanate following the death of Ahmad bin Sa'id in 1783. The Al Saud moved against Zubara immediately after their capture of al-Hasa in 1795. In a last-ditch effort to thwart the advance of the Al Saud, Shaikh Sulman bin Ahmad and his followers abandoned Zubara for more defensible positions on al-Awal, hoping the invaders would retire to al-Hasa when they found no booty in the city. This strategy seems to have had some success, as the Al Saud turned their attention northward toward Kuwait and southern Iraq and did not press on to attack Bahrain. But Zubara was not reoccupied by the Al Khalifah until 1799, and by the early 1800s control of the area had become contested by the Al Thani and Al Sudan, allies of the Al Saud based at Doha on the eastern coast of the Qatar peninsula.

Relations between the Al Khalifah and the Al Saud improved significantly at the turn of the century in response to the threat posed to Bahrain from the imam of Muscat. In 1799, Omani forces raided the islands, charging that Bahraini ships were refusing to pay the tolls levied on vessels passing through the Strait of Hormuz. The following year, a larger expedition overran al-Awal and took 26 prominent local families hostage to force the Al Khalifah to pay tribute to the imam's treasury. Shaikh Sulman appealed to 'Abd al-'Aziz Al Saud for assistance, and an army made up of Bani 'Utub from Bahrain and Kuwait and Muwahhidin from al-Hasa succeeded in recapturing Manama in 1801. When the Omani ruler again moved against the islands a year later, the Al Saud sent an expeditionary force south toward the hinterlands of Muscat itself, compelling the imam to break off the attack.

Attempts by each of these two outside powers to take over the archipelago continued intermittently throughout the next two decades. In the spring of 1810, an Omani task force once again raided Bahrain and then moved on to Zubara, routing the defenders and setting fire to the town. In response, the governor of al-Hasa dispatched one of his field commanders to al-Awal and reinforced the Muwahhidin garrisons in both Bahrain and Qatar. But when these troops were recalled to Najd in 1811 to counter movements by Egyptian forces on the borders of the Hijaz, the imam renewed the attack and recaptured Bahrain, withdrawing only after Shaikhs Sulman and 'Abdullah agreed to pay an annual tribute to Muscat. Repeated raids by the Muwahhidin on the eastern marches of Oman during the course of the next two years failed to end Omani hegemony over the islands. At the end of 1819, a joint Persian-Omani expedition to conquer Bahrain once and for all was deterred from setting out when the two shuyukhs of the Al Khalifah persuaded the commander of the British fleet operating off Ras al-Khaimah to extend them protection as signatories of the 1820 General Treaty of Peace. The following spring the imam informed the British admiral that an expedition against the islands had become superfluous, as the Al Khalifah had renewed their promise to pay tribute to his government. A final Omani offensive against Bahrain was launched in August 1828 with the assistance of the Bani Yas of Abu Dhabi, but it was repelled after a fierce battle at Jufair. When British officials refused to mediate an end to the conflict, the shaikh of Bushire stepped in and arranged for the imam formally to abandon all claim to the islands in December 1829.

BRITISH POLICY IN THE GULF
AND AL KHALIFAH RULE

British diplomacy buttressed Al Khalifah sovereignty in four interrelated ways during the course of the nineteenth century. In the first place, Great Britain selected a limited number of chiefs and made them responsible for maintaining order along the southern Gulf littoral. This process enhanced the authority and prestige of the leaders and families chosen and promoted them from their traditional position as shuyukh, or primus inter pares among their more influential supporters, to a role more closely approximating that of ruler of an established community (hakim).[11] Second, British representatives imposed an end to interclan warfare in the region, perceiving these actions as threats to British and Indian commerce. Thus the imperial government in Bombay set out in 1819 to eradicate what it called large-scale "piracy" along the Gulf coast from al-Hasa to Oman. Although the Al Khalifah had not engaged in raids on outside shipping, British officials considered the islands' ports clearing houses for hijacked goods and forced Shaikhs Sulman and 'Abdullah to sign the General Treaty of Peace circulated among the Arab rulers of the Gulf the following year. Subsequent treaties reinforced the authority of the Al Khalifah in general and of later rulers in particular.

Third, the imperial administration of India, unwilling to tolerate the fluid boundaries among tribes that characterized the region, insisted on demarcating the limits of each ruling family's territory. This trend became more pronounced during the first third of the twentieth century, when oil companies began negotiating for concessions in the Gulf, but it was evident in earlier decades as well. Finally, in the course of negotiating with these rulers, British enterprises awarded subsidies and rents in exchange for access to local territory. These contracts provided the leaders of dominant clans such as the Al Khalifah with sufficient resources to allow them to act autonomously of their richer "subjects," overturning the symbiotic relationship that had existed between the tribal aristocracy and the merchant oligarchy in previous centuries.[12]

Beginning in the first decade of the nineteenth century, British officials recognized the Al Khalifah as the party accountable for activities undertaken by Bahrain's inhabitants. This policy cemented the family's predominance over the country's internal and external affairs. From 1820 to 1904, political conflict on the islands consisted primarily of internecine rivalry within the ruling family rather than challenges to Al Khalifah authority on the part of other forces. Muhammad al-Rumaihi reports that in the years after the conquest of Bahrain "the Al-Khalifah adopted a system of dual rulership; the father being assisted during his lifetime by two of his sons and on his death the two sons continued with their duties and shared all authority."[13] Thus Shaikh Sulman bin Ahmad took charge of Manama in the years after 1796, while his brother Shaikh 'Abdullah ruled Muharraq. These two factions competed with one another for wealth and power during the 1820s and 1830s, with both leaders levying increased taxes upon the merchants and farmers residing in their respective domains and Shaikh 'Abdullah launching a series of raids on the port cities of eastern Arabia controlled by the Muwahhidin. The disorder that attended these actions seriously disrupted local trade and led a number of subordinate tribes to emigrate to other parts of the Gulf. They also led Shaikh Sulman's grandson, Muhammad bin Khalifah, to ask for the assistance of the allies of the Al Saud in ousting his great uncle; and with the aid of the Al Bin 'Ali, Al Jalahima, and other forces based in Qatar, he was finally able to defeat Shaikh 'Abdullah and drive his followers into exile at Dammam. Attempts by the old shaikh to retake Muharraq were blocked by the intervention of British and Muwahhidin forces between 1843 and 1846.

Periodic conflict between the two branches of the Al Khalifah persisted through the 1850s and early 1860s, with the successors of Shaikh 'Abdullah forming a coalition with the Muwahhidin of both al-Hasa and Qatar in an effort to unseat their cousins in Manama. When Shaikh Muhammad bin Khalifah attacked his opponents' home bases at Doha and Wakrah on the Qatari coast in the fall of 1867, British officials finally sent a three-ship flotilla to impose an end to the fighting. Under the terms exacted of Shaikh Muhammad's brother by the British commander, all of the warships owned by the Al Khalifah were burned, the main fort at Muharraq was razed, and a substantial sum was given to the residents of Doha and Wakrah as reparations. But this intervention only pushed Shaikh Muhammad into a temporary alliance with 'Abdullah's grandson Nasir, whose combined forces invaded Bahrain two years later and pillaged Manama before reestablishing residence at Muharraq.

In November 1869 a second British task force took control of the islands and exiled the leaders of both factions to India. As a way of ending the rivalry once and for all, the imperial government in Bombay appointed Shaikh 'Isa bin 'Ali, who was in charge of the Al Khalifah's remaining holdings in Qatar, as ruler. It was with Shaikh 'Isa that the British Resident concluded a formal treaty in December 1880, following a decade of diplomatic alarms and military excursions along the coasts of eastern Arabia, in which the ruler as "Chief of Bahrain" pledged to "bind myself and successors . . . to abstain from entering into negotiations or making treaties of any sort with any State or Government other than the British without the consent of the said British Government."[14] This document was superseded by a second signed in March 1892, in which Shaikh 'Isa promised "that I will on no account cede, sell, mortgage or otherwise give for occupation, any part of my territory save to the British Government." The upshot of these agreements was that the shuyukh of the Al Khalifah gained an indisputable position at the apex of Bahraini politics, from which neither merchant discontent nor tribal defections could easily dislodge him.

Although the treaties of 1880 and 1892 proved crucial in buttressing the predominant position of the shuyukh of the Al Khalifah within Bahraini society, they were not the most significant arrangements concluded between the local rulers and British agents as far as the Indian administration was concerned. Officials in Bombay had an overriding interest in expanding the level of Indian trade passing through the Gulf and feared that any disruption of long-distance commerce in this region would work to the benefit of indigenous traders. As part of its effort to support the operations of Indian merchants, British officers suppressed the more aggressive of their local rivals and cowed them into signing a General Treaty of Maritime Peace by destroying the port and navy of Hasan bin Rahma Al Qasimi at Ras al-Khaimah at the end of 1819. The co-rulers of Bahrain, who had attempted to mediate between the Qawasim and the British, were included among the signatories of this treaty.

Because the General Treaty of 1820 allowed local rulers to attack the shipping of any rivals upon whom they had declared a state of war, this first compact did little to reduce the general level of maritime conflict in the Gulf. The acting British Resident at Bushire attempted to plug the most gaping holes in the document in 1835, by proposing a general truce whereby all signatories would agree to refrain from attacking one another's shipping during the pearling season and would limit all future operations to the southern side of the Gulf. This truce proved more effective than its predecessor and was gradually extended into a Treaty of Peace in Perpetuity, concluded in May 1853. The rulers of Bahrain were consciously excluded from any of these later accords, on the grounds that their participation would commit the British empire to defending the islands not only from other shuyukhs but from the rulers of Shiraz, Muscat and al-Hasa as well.

Three episodes persuaded the imperial government in Bombay to include Bahrain within an expanded trucial system despite Persian, Omani, and Muwahhidini claims to the islands. In the spring of 1839, Egyptian forces under the command of Khurshid Pasha were in firm possession of al-Hasa and had begun to sponsor attempts by their local allies to take control of Sharjah and the forts guarding the oasis at Buraimi. British officials feared that the ultimate goal of this expedition was the conquest of Bahrain, from which position the Egyptian ruler, Muhammad 'Ali Pasha, could threaten to move against Kuwait, Basra, and Oman. These fears grew when Shaikh 'Abdullah bin Ahmad secretly agreed to submit to Egyptian suzerainty and pay an annual tribute to Cairo in exchange for recognition as sole ruler of Bahrain and assurances that the territories claimed by the Al Khalifah in Qatar would be left untouched.

Shaikh 'Abdullah's action threatened to undermine British hegemony in the region and encourage a resumption of "piracy and maritime warfare" in Gulf waters. When the acting Resident at Bushire attempted to persuade the ruler of Muscat to assist in stopping Khurshid Pasha and restoring order to the Gulf littoral, the sultan replied that the British should send an expeditionary force of their own to occupy Bahrain. Sayyid Sa'id went on to say that if the imperial administration would not carry out such an operation, he would. The Resident reported to his superiors in Bombay that under the circumstances occupying the islands might be a good idea: Annexing Bahrain "would secure to Britain a preponderating influence in Gulf politics" and would insure that the sultan would make no effort to annex the territory for himself.[15] But before the imperial government had a chance to decide whether or not to launch such an expedition, the Egyptian army withdrew to the Hijaz, and Britain's ascendency in the Gulf survived intact.

Forty years later, renewed fighting between the Al Khalifah and various parties based on the Arabian mainland prompted direct intervention on the part of British officers to separate the combatants. In November 1878 the combined forces of Nasir bin Mubarak Al Khalifah and Shaikh Qasim bin Muhammad Al Thani razed Zubara. The British Resident at Bushire elected not to relieve the garrison of Na'im tribesmen loyal to the Al Khalifah, besieged in a fort on the edge of town, despite repeated appeals from Shaikh 'Isa for him honor the terms of an 1861 treaty, in which Britain pledged to protect the security and independence of Al Khalifah possessions. Instead, this officer arranged for an Ottoman gunboat to bring the fighting to an end and proposed that the Turkish governor of al-Hasa establish a permanent outpost at the town. This move only exacerbated Shaikh 'Isa's fears that the islands were being left open to invasion. Two months later, tribespeople based on the mainland began plundering Bahraini ships and raiding coastal settlements around al-Awal. Shaikh 'Isa requested permission to launch strikes against Dhahran to punish the attackers but was "strictly forbidden to do so, and was told that the British would 'look after his interests' and prevent such piratical attacks."[16]

At this point the Bahraini ruler undertook a number of covert operations to protect the islands from his opponents on the mainland. He began secret negotiations with the Ottoman governors of Basra and al-Hasa to permit their armed forces access to facilities on al-Awal in exchange for their assistance in suppressing the descendants of Shaikh 'Abdullah and their allies. He set up an extensive network of spies in the towns around the Qatari peninsula to monitor the activities of the dissident Bani Hajir and the Al Thani. And he dispatched small raiding parties to destroy boats at settlements up and down the Arabian coast before they could be commandeered by his rivals. These actions alarmed British officials, who worried that continued unrest in Qatar would lead to an expansion of Ottoman influence in the region. Consequently, the Resident included as part of the treaty of 1880 a clause obligating Shaikh 'Isa to refuse permission to set up local installations to any outside power without British consent and prohibiting the ruler from engaging in any but "friendly" relations concerning "business of minor importance" with his neighbors.[17] But even this language turned out to be insufficient to prevent subsequent skirmishes between the Al Khalifah and their enemies on the mainland.

In early 1895, Shaikh Sultan bin Salama Al Bin 'Ali pulled his followers out of Bahrain in reaction to a quarrel with senior members of the Al Khalifah. The Al Thani, after a half-hearted attempt on the part of Shaikh Qasim to mediate the dispute, invited the emigrants to settle at Zubara; in May, the Ottoman governor of al-Hasa ordered a contingent of Turkish troops and engineers to assist in rebuilding the town and called on the Bani Hajir to relocate their main encampment to an adjacent site. These actions led Shaikh 'Isa and the British Resident at Bushire to issue warnings to the Al Bin 'Ali to evacuate the area or face confiscation of the fleet belonging to the clan. When Shaikh Sultan refused to acknowledge these warnings, the commander of the British flotilla operating in the Gulf seized 16 of the Al Bin 'Ali's boats and towed them to Manama. In retaliation, the Ottoman garrison at Zubara confiscated a number of Bahraini vessels, while Shaikh Qasim ordered boats owned by the Al Thani to return from the pearling banks and prepare for military action.

Tension mounted during July, when an Ottoman warship moved into position off the coast, and the local authorities began calling for the overthrow of the Al Khalifah. In mid-August, the governor of al-Hasa declared that he could no longer be responsible for any actions undertaken by the tribes of Qatar and that these forces intended to attack Bahrain if the Al Bin 'Ali's fleet was not released by early September. Fearing the worst, the commander of the British task force sailed for Zubara on 5 September and found a group of ships being outfitted for a raid on the islands. Without receiving orders from Bombay, he ordered his warships to destroy the Qatari fleet. This show of force convinced Shaikh Qasim to sue for peace; the British accepted his surrender on condition that the Al Bin 'Ali return to Bahrain, the Ottoman forces evacuate Zubara, and the Al Thani pay 30,000 rupees ($15,000) to the Indian government. As the imperial viceroy of India observed later, "the whole incident was minor: but a precedent had been set, and Britain had interfered directly and in a forceful manner in mainland affairs— even to the point . . . of disciplining an Ottoman qaimaqam."[18] More important, at least from the perspective of the Al Khalifah, this incident led directly to the appointment of a British Political Agent on the islands five years later.

Imposing an end to interclan warfare along the Gulf littoral entailed demarcating the territorial boundaries within which each shuyukh in the area could exercise legitimate authority. Prior to 1880, few if any clearly defined political boundaries existed in the Gulf region. In the words of Peter Lienhardt, "Only according to very limited criteria could any one shaykhdom of the Gulf be counted as a discrete, self-sufficient political entity. For the most part, the workings of internal politics have to be seen in relation to engagements, actual or potential, with other shaykhdoms."[19] Conflicts among dominant clans, as well as defections across tribal coalitions, shifted from place to place as communities themselves moved from settlement to settlement. Thus, from 1843 to 1846 Shaikh 'Abdullah bin Ahmad attempted to attract allies to help him recapture Bahrain first at Dammam, then at Naband on the Persian coast, then at Qatif, then at Tarut Island off the coast of al-Hasa and finally at Fuwairat on the Qatar peninsula. And the ambiguous status of Zubara created perennial difficulties for both the Al Khalifah and their de facto protectors, the British government of India, throughout the century.

In the years after 1860, British authorities in the Gulf put increasing pressure on the rulers of Bahrain to limit their authority to the islands themselves and relinquish all claim to possessions on the Arabian coast. Successive Residents strongly advised the leaders of the Al Khalifah to avoid entangling themselves in affairs on the mainland, although senior officials in the Bombay administration avoided taking a clear position on the "complicated" issue of which territories the clan had a legitimate right to govern. When the Resident in 1874 gave Shaikh 'Isa permission to reinforce Zubara as a defensive measure, the Indian government censured him, claiming that previous correspondence had demonstrated "that the Chief of Bahrein had no *possessions* on the mainland of Gutter, and that his rights were of a very uncertain character."[20] This action, in effect, denied the Al Khalifah's long-standing claim to the area around Zubara and put the ruler on notice that British forces would do nothing to defend that territory from Ottoman or Qatari encroachment. By the fall of 1878, the Indian administration was ordering its flotilla in the Gulf to support Turkish efforts to maintain order along the coast of the peninsula and ignoring Shaikh 'Isa's requests to be allowed to carry out operations of his own to suppress piracy in the region.

British officials continued to restrain the Al Khalifah from intervening in Qatari affairs during the next 40 years. When the Ottoman government announced that it planned to set up administrative posts at Zubara and Doha in the spring of 1903, the Indian authorities responded by proposing that a British protectorate be created on the peninsula; this proposal was vetoed by the government in London. Ten years later, following the outbreak of war in the Balkans, Turkish authorities entered into negotiations with British representatives to determine the disposition of territories all along the Gulf littoral. These negotiations resulted in an Anglo-Ottoman accord signed in July 1913, in which the British agreed to prevent Shaikh 'Isa from attempting to annex any portion of the Qatar peninsula, an area recognized as the legitimate domain of the Al Thani. The resurgence of the Muwahhidin in al-Hasa that summer prompted officials in both Bombay and London to keep an even tighter rein on Shaikh 'Isa to insure the preservation of Bahraini neutrality in the event of war between Ottoman forces and the Al Saud. With the coming of World War I, the Resident at Bushire concluded an agreement with Shaikh Qasim committing the British to the defense of Qatar from external attack. This treaty effectively terminated Al Khalifah involvement in political affairs on the peninsula.

Along with demarcation of each country's territorial boundaries came a variety of subsidies paid out by British concerns for the right to operate safely within that ruler's domain. The first enterprise whose operations injected a regular flow of monies into local treasuries was the British India Steam Navigation Company, which—under a subsidy from the Indian administration—inaugurated steamship service in the Gulf in 1862 to carry mail between Basra and Bombay by way of Karachi.[21] The company appointed shipping agents at each of its ports of call, Bahrain being the only one located on the southern shore of the Gulf during the nineteenth century. This representative was responsible for obtaining any local customs permits, for supervising the off-loading and storage of cargo, and for inspecting shipments to make sure they contained no prohibited items, such as firearms and gunpowder. In Bahrain, the company agent also played a major part in marketing locally produced pearls overseas. The number of British India steamers calling on the islands averaged around 15 per year during the mid-1870s, but jumped to 45 in 1879; for the next 10 years there was a steady rise in such calls: from 29 in 1882 to 56 in 1892. The peak of company operations was reached in 1869–1889, when the number of British steamships calling at Bahrain exceeded those at any of the other Gulf ports. The Al Khalifah profited handsomely from the fees paid by this firm to facilitate its local activities.

More specific in their benefits, however, were the contracts undertaken by Bahrain's rulers with the local representatives of international petroleum companies. In December 1925, the agent for a small oil-exploration syndicate, Major Frank Holmes, was granted a three-year concession to explore 100,000 acres (40,000 hectares) on al-Awal in exchange for annual payments to Shaikh Hamad of 10,000 rupees ($5,000), plus a substantial bonus if oil were discovered. Holmes was unable to convince any of the British firms operating in the Gulf to purchase his concession but ultimately found a buyer in Standard Oil Company of California, which contracted with the ruler in August 1930 to drill a set of exploratory wells in the central part of the island. In return, the company agreed to pay Shaikh Hamad a royalty of more than 3 rupees ($1.50) for every ton of petroleum produced, or a minimum of 75,000 rupees ($37,500) per year, for the next 55 years. In July 1940, after oil in commercial quantities had been found on the islands, Standard Oil and its new partner, the Texas Oil Company, signed a revised concession with the ruler, according to whose terms Shaikh Hamad was given an advance of £30,000 ($150,000) and minimum annual royalty payments of £95,000 ($475,000) for the succeeding 15 years. These monies went directly into the ruler's personal treasury, upsetting what Rosemarie Said Zahlan has called the "state of economic interdependence between the ruler and his community" that had existed in Bahrain prior to this time.[22] In other words, the royalties from oil production provided the shuyukh of the Al Khalifah with a regular income, independent of trends in the commercial and agricultural sectors of the islands' economy.

At about the same time Shaikh Hamad was negotiating with Standard Oil of California, he undertook equally significant partnerships with the Royal Air Force (RAF) and its commercial adjunct, Imperial Airways. The former began making occasional use of a landing field outside Muharraq in the mid-1920s and made a detailed reconnaissance of the islands in the spring of 1929. At that time, the RAF's 203rd (Flying Boat) Squadron acquired an abandoned quarantine station southeast of Manama as a rest house, laid out a landing site in the vicinity of the ruler's palace, and arranged for "a local firm" to take care of refueling.[23] Under the terms of the agreement reached with Shaikh Hamad for the use of these facilities, the ruler accepted full responsibility for protecting the rest house and landing field in exchange for payments to cover the expense of hiring guards, maintaining the buildings, and leasing the property. As Zahlan has observed, this agreement made the ruler an active, rather than a passive, partner with British officials in the region: Should he or his successors decide to renege on the bargain, vital and expensive facilities would be endangered.[24] Consequently, Britain's local representatives offered substantial compensation to insure that the terms of the agreement regarding air transport would be carried out.

THE COMING OF BRITISH
IMPERIAL ADMINISTRATION

Commercial activity increased dramatically throughout the Gulf during the last quarter of the nineteenth century. At Bahrain, the value of imports coming into the islands rose from almost 2.3 million rupees ($1.15 million) to more than 8.8 million rupees ($2.9 million) between 1878 and 1899; the value of exports increased from almost 2.2 million rupees ($1.1 million) to just over 7.9 million rupees ($2.6 million) in the same period. This trend brought an influx of Indian (or Banian) merchants into the area, who specialized in the import and reexport of cloth manufactured on the subcontinent and in providing loans to smaller local traders. The commercial expansion of the late 1800s also attracted European firms into the Gulf in growing numbers: The most notorious of these were Robert Woenckhaus and Company, which opened a branch office at Manama in December 1900, and the partnership of the French entrepreneur Goguyer and the Hasawi Muhammad bin 'Abd al-Wahhab, whom the British suspected of dealing in arms. But other actors also joined the rush to find a place in the Gulf sun: In 1901 the Russians set up a consulate-general at Bushire and a consulate at Basra to encourage trade with the region but ended up having to rely on an established Dutch firm to carry on the limited amount of business these consuls generated. Consequently, the turn of the century represented a period of serious rivalry among a number of European and Indian camps for a predominant share in regional trade.

As the amount of commerce passing through Manama grew, Bahraini merchants became increasingly discontented with the prerogatives held by the islands' Banian traders and their local partners. Britain's native agent on the islands reported to the Resident at Bushire in the fall of 1882 that established houses in the city were only deterred from sponsoring physical attacks on their Banian competitors by the likelihood of British retaliation.[25] The native agent himself was a Persian merchant with Ottoman citizenship, whose relations with Shaikh 'Isa and others of the Al Khalifah were cool at best; thus he was largely unable to protect British subjects from unfair trading practices in the local marketplace. Moreover, the agent entered into partnership with a local firm engaged in running guns between the Persian coast and eastern Arabia at a time when the imperial government in Bombay was doing its best to suppress the arms trade in the Gulf as part of its campaign to pacify the North-West Frontier of India. When Shaikh 'Isa's son traveled to Bushire in November 1897 to obtain the Resident's imprimatur as heir apparent, officials in Bombay demanded in return that control over the customs at the port of Manama be turned over to an officer—preferably from the outside—appointed by the British authorities.

Shaikh 'Isa bridled at this attempt to reform the customs at Bahrain's major port and managed to postpone any action on this matter for seven years. Meanwhile, more and more disputes between foreign nationals and the local population arose. As a result, a succession of outside concerns made overtures to the Al Khalifah concerning the administration of the customs: In August 1901 a delegation of Belgian experts visited Manama, having just been contracted to help reform the Persian customs, and asked if it could be of any assistance to Shaikh 'Isa; Russian and French agents arrived on the islands to make similar inquiries during the next two years. By 1904 the Indian government concluded that customs reform could be delayed no longer, and the newly assigned Resident at Bushire, Major Percy Cox, was instructed to "take the Customs question in hand."[26] In August of that year, the India Office in London approved the stationing of a graded Political Officer at Manama, with a guard of sepoys to provide both security and muscle for the outpost.

Before the Indian administration could appoint an officer to this position, a string of serious disorders broke out in Manama. Supporters of the governor of the city, Shaikh 'Ali bin Ahmad, chafing at Shaikh Hamad's investiture as heir apparent, initiated a series of lootings of shops and warehouses in the local *suq* (marketplace). In late September, a group of Shaikh 'Ali's retainers set upon an Arab employee of Woenckhaus and injured a second (German) employee trying to protect him. Talal Farah observes that this incident was rooted in the German firm's refusal to pay off the governor's associates and its ability to bypass the cargo fleet maintained by the Al Khalifah.[27] Shaikh 'Isa hesitated to impose retribution on a senior member of the ruling family and protested to the Resident at Bushire that Woenckhaus had misrepresented the facts of the case. Cox being unavailable at the time, the newly arrived Political Agent in Manama took it upon himself to render judgment upon the parties concerned; his decision to require an apology of Shaikh 'Ali and a month's imprisonment of his retainers satisfied no one.

In mid-November a similar incident took place, this time precipitated by a fight between an employee of the most prominent member of the city's Persian community and one of Shaikh 'Ali's black servants. Promising to indemnify the Persian, who had charge of off-loading all cargo at the Manama docks, Shaikh 'Isa referred the case to the Sunni *shari'a* court of the city's principal *qadi*, Shaikh Qasim (who had himself taken part in the ruckus on the side of Shaikh 'Ali's partisans). By this means, the ruler hoped to drive a wedge between the city's commercial Sunni elite and the dissident faction within the Al Khalifah. The British Agent, however, objected that no Sunni court could be expected to provide justice to Persian Shi'i, particularly if senior members of the ruling family were involved. Instead, he insisted that Shaikh 'Ali's servant should be "soundly flogged" and that Shaikh 'Ali himself should be deported; he then called in a British gunboat to back up his demand. When none of the local population volunteered to carry out the flogging, a sailor from the British warship was ordered to do so. But Shaikh 'Isa adamantly refused to exile his nephew, considering this demand a challenge to his prerogatives as ruler.

Upon conferring with his superiors in Bombay, Cox returned to the islands in late February 1905 at the head of a three-ship flotilla and repeated his subordinate's demand that Shaikh 'Ali be deported. After three days of tense bargaining, Shaikh 'Isa capitulated and turned over to the Resident the property of his nephew (who had escaped from the island in the middle of the negotiations) as well as the ringleaders of the assault on the Persian's employee. This act failed to propitiate Cox, who subsequently advised the imperial government to appoint a governor for Manama and relegate Shaikh 'Isa to the largely ceremonial post of governor of Muharraq Island. Bombay refrained from implementing so drastic a measure and ordered the Resident to continue to monitor activities at the port to insure that trade was not interrupted by local wrangling. By the end of the decade, regional commerce had grown, and receipts from local customs had increased, so the issue evaporated.

In the years after 1905, British officials appropriated greater and greater degrees of jurisdiction over Bahrain's commercial affairs by placing increasing numbers of foreigners under the consular authority of the Political Agent at Manama. There existed little legal basis for this development until November 1907, when the Indian government adopted an Order in Council that would codify the judicial powers of the Political Agent regarding foreign nationals residing on the islands. This order was debated in London for the next eight years, as the government attempted to sort out the relationship between European diplomatic affairs and German and Ottoman moves in the Gulf region. By the time the order was proclaimed in early 1919, not only had the Political Agent become the de facto arbiter of commercial disputes within the country, but the ruler had promised to obtain British approval before offering any party a concession to explore for oil at the promising site around Jabal ad-Dukhan as well.

THE CONSOLIDATION OF AL KHALIFAH RULE

In November 1919, Major H.R.P. Dickson arrived in Manama to become the second Political Agent assigned to the islands. Dickson perceived the existing state of affairs to be "wholly unsatisfactory," as there was in Bahrain "a strong anti-British sentiment which is long-standing and deepseated," and "British prestige rests on entirely false standards, namely on fear and not on respect."[28] He set about to change this situation by implementing a series of reforms in the local admin-istration: During the summer of 1920, he convened a reconstituted Municipal Council for Manama, composed of four members appointed by the ruler and four designated by the Agent, to supervise public health, traffic, and other matters; he then abolished the existing system of private guards having allegiance to senior Al Khalifah shaikhs and replaced it with a civil guard under the command of the Municipal

Council; toward the end of the year, he announced that British protection would be extended to "all foreign subjects including Persians and subjects of Arab rulers and chiefs other than those of Bahrain" residing on the islands; finally, he set up a reformed Customary Council (Majlis al-'Urf), five of whose members were appointed by the ruler and five by the Agent, to settle disputes involving the country's merchants. These measures aroused opposition not only from within the Al Khalifah, whose members felt they undermined the family's customary authority, but also from the islands' commercial elite, whose members saw in them an effort to give unfair advantage to non-Bahrainis. Moreover, the country's Shi'i community, sensing that the Agent's actions were undermining the position of the Al Khalifah, seized the opportunity to demand an end to forced labor and the more onerous taxes imposed upon it by the regime.

Dickson was replaced at the end of 1920 by Major Clive K. Daly, who had served as a regional military governor in Iraq during the rebellion of 1918–1920. Daly adopted a tough-minded approach to carrying out the reforms Dickson had proposed that did little to dampen local discontent. In November 1921, he deported Qasim ash-Shirawi— a prominent merchant and director of the port at Muharraq—for organizing a drive to petition the Indian government to rescind the reforms; then he replaced the head of the Manama Municipal Council, who was outspoken in his criticism of the reforms, with the more accommodating Shaikh Hamad bin 'Isa. Finally, the Agent appointed a leading Persian merchant as secretary of the municipality and head of the city's force of market police. This last move alienated the indigenous commercial oligarchy, particularly when it was rumored that the new secretary was recruiting Persians to staff the police corps.

As the Al Khalifah's position in local society continued to deteriorate, senior shaikhs in charge of the family's estates began to exact greater levels of taxation from their predominantly Shi'i laborers. The Shi'a appealed to the Political Agent for redress of their grievances and relief from further exploitation. In response, Daly extended British protection to a number of indigenous Shi'is most seriously injured by Sunni tribespeople. This policy raised the degree of animosity between those who benefited from the reforms and those—notably the leading shaikhs and established merchants—who did not. Hostility between the two factions was heightened when the Persian press began openly criticizing British interference in the islands' affairs in the summer of 1922 and the Foreign Office in London responded by recommending that the Agent take "steps   to ensure the equitable treatment of Shi'a" as a way of defusing Persian criticism.[29] The tension generated by these developments precipitated a series of riots on the islands in May 1923, followed by attacks on Shi'i villages on al-Awal and Sitra by Sunni tribespeople of the Dawasir and Al Khalifah.

Bombay immediately dispatched two gunboats under the command of the acting Resident at Bushire, Lieutenant-Colonel S. G. Knox, to restore order in Bahrain. By the end of May, Knox had invested Shaikh Hamad with responsibility for "the active conduct of affairs" on the islands, deported a leading member of the Sunni tribal population who had attempted to establish contact with the Al Saud and exiled to India a handful of the most prominent local merchants who had opposed the reforms.[30] In addition, he demanded on 21 May that Shaikh 'Isa abdicate in favor of Shaikh Hamad, but the old ruler refused to do so until he had consulted the tribes. When the process of consultation began to drag on, the Resident called a congress of the islands' leaders and announced that power had been transferred to Shaikh Hamad. He then ordered all customs revenues to be deposited at the local branch of the Eastern Bank as government property and brought in an official of the Indian customs service to supervise the administration of the country's ports.

Following the conclusion of the pearling season, a group of prominent Sunni merchants convened a "national congress" and selected twelve representatives to present a list of counterdemands to the Political Agent. The most important of these demands were that Shaikh 'Isa be reinstated as ruler, unless he voluntarily stepped aside in favor of his son; that a consultative council composed of both Sunni and Shi'i delegates be formed to assist in governing the country; and that a committee of four individuals with experience in the pearling industry be appointed to serve as a divers' court. The Resident traveled to Bahrain in early November and asked to meet with the representatives of the congress to discuss their proposals; when they arrived at the Agency house, however, he arrested two of their leaders and deported them to India, apparently with the help of Shaikh Hamad. Furthermore, Knox ordered the Dawasir—whose members had again attacked the Shi'i town of 'Ali in mid-May—to leave the islands, following which he confiscated the clan's property around al-Budayya' and assigned ownership to the local administration.

These moves broke the opposition to the reforms carried out by the British authorities, although acts of violence against both the Shi'a and the new regime continued sporadically over the next two years. In the summer of 1924, the Agent engaged a Briton to serve as permanent adviser to the ruler. With the arrival of this official, Charles D. Belgrave, at Manama on 31 March 1926, both the paramount position of Shaikh Hamad and the stability of the emerging imperial order on the islands—whereby the adviser was in charge of all branches of the local administration, assisted by a small corps of British civil servants—were assured. As a visitor to Bahrain reported back to his fellows at the Central Asia Society in London in 1929, the shaikhdom "is not a protectorate, but under British advice has achieved very considerable progress. Life and property are now safe, and the Shaikh employs three Englishmen who are respectively employed in managing his revenue, his customs, and his police. Indeed, conditions are fully comparable with a well-run Indian state."[31]

NOTES

1. Christopher Edens, "Bahrain and the Arabian Gulf During the Second Millennium B.C.: Urban Crisis and Colonialism," in Shaikha Haya Ali Al Khalifa and Michael Rice, eds., *Bahrain Through the Ages: The Archaeology* (London: KPI, 1986); Michael Rice, "'Dilmun Discovered'—The Archaeology of Bahrain to the Early Second Millenium BC," *Asian Affairs* (London) 17(October 1986), pp. 252–263; Michael Rice, *Search for the Paradise Land* (London: Longman, 1985).

2. Gerd Weisgerber, "Dilmun—A Trading Entrepot: Evidence from Historical and Archaeological Sources," in Al Khalifa and Rice, *Bahrain Through the Ages*.

3. G. W. Bowersock, "Tylos and Tyre: Bahrain in the Graeco-Roman World," in Al Khalifa and Rice, *Bahrain Through the Ages*.

4. Richard N. Frye, "Bahrain Under the Sasanians," in Daniel T. Potts, ed., *Dilmun: New Studies in the Archaeology and Early History of Bahrain* (Berlin: Dietrich Reimer Verlag, 1983).

5. Elias S. Shoufani, *Al-Riddah and the Muslim Conquest of Arabia* (Toronto: University of Toronto Press, 1973); George Rentz and W. E. Mulligan, "Al-Bahrayn," *The Encyclopedia of Islam*, second edition (Leiden: E. J. Brill, 1952); Safa Khulusi, "A Thirteenth Century Poet from Bahrain," Proceedings of the Ninth Seminar for Arabian Studies, School of Oriental and African Studies, University of London, July 1975; James H. D. Belgrave, "A Brief Survey of the History of the Bahrain Islands," *Asian Affairs* (London) 39(January 1952), pp. 57–68.

6. Andrew Williamson, "Hurmuz and the Trade of the Gulf in the 14th and 15th Centuries A.D.," Proceedings of the Sixth Seminar for Arabian Studies, Institute of Archaeology, London, September 1972.

7. Salih Ozbaran, "The Ottoman Turks and the Portuguese in the Persian Gulf, 1534–1581," *Journal of Asian History* 6(1972), pp. 45–87; A. W. Stiffe, "Ancient Trading Centres of the Persian Gulf: VII. Bahrein," *Geographical Journal* 18(September 1901), pp. 291–294; Charles D. Belgrave, "The Portuguese in the Bahrain Islands, 1521–1602," *Journal of the Royal Central Asian Society* 22(October 1935), pp. 617–630.

8. Belgrave, "Portuguese," pp. 628–629.

9. Abdul Amir Amin, *British Interests in the Persian Gulf* (Leiden: E. J. Brill, 1967), pp. 29–33, 49.

10. Ahmad Abu Hakima, *History of Eastern Arabia: The Rise and Development of Bahrain and Kuwait* (Beirut: Khayats, 1965).

11. See J. E. Peterson, "Tribes and Politics in Eastern Arabia," *Middle East Journal* 31(Summer 1977), pp. 297–312.

12. Peter Lienhardt, "The Authority of Shaykhs in the Gulf: An Essay in Nineteenth-Century History," in R. B. Serjeant and R. L. Bidwell, eds., *Arabian Studies*, volume 2 (London: C. Hurst, 1975).

13. Mohammed Ghanim al-Rumaihi, *Bahrain: A Study on Social and Political Changes Since the First World War* (Kuwait: University of Kuwait Press, 1975), p. 5.

14. Briton Cooper Busch, *Britain and the Persian Gulf, 1894–1914* (Berkeley: University of California Press, 1967), p. 27.

15. J. B. Kelly, "Mehemet 'Ali's Expedition to the Persian Gulf 1837–1840, Part II," *Middle Eastern Studies* 2(October 1965), pp. 42–43.

16. Talal Toufic Farah, *Protection and Politics in Bahrain 1869–1915* (Beirut: American University of Beirut Press, 1985), p. 61.

17. Ibid., p. 66.

18. Busch, *Britain and the Persian Gulf*, p. 136.

19. Lienhardt, "Authority of Shaykhs," p. 74.

20. Farah, *Protection and Politics*, pp. 47, 51.

21. Stephanie Jones, "The Management of British India Steamers in the Gulf 1862–1945," in R. I. Lawless, ed., *The Gulf in the Early 20th. Century*, Centre for Middle Eastern and Islamic Studies, University of Durham, Occasional Papers Series, No. 31(1986).

22. Rosemarie Said Zahlan, "The Impact of the Early Oil Concessions in the Gulf States," in Lawless, *The Gulf in the Early 20th. Century*, p. 72.

23. G. W. Bentley, "The Development of the Air Route in the Persian Gulf," *Journal of the Royal Central Asian Society* 20(April 1933), p. 178.

24. Zahlan, "Impact of the Early Oil Concessions," p. 65.

25. Farah, *Protection and Politics*, p. 73.

26. Ibid., p. 126.

27. Ibid., p. 132.

28. Al-Rumaihi, *Bahrain*, p. 230.

29. Ibid., p. 240.

30. Fuad I. Khuri, *Tribe and State in Bahrain* (Chicago: University of Chicago Press, 1980), p. 95.

31. Lionel Haworth, "Persia and the Persian Gulf," *Journal of the Central Asian Society* 16(1929), p. 502.

3

The Nationalist Movements of the 1950s

From the mid-1930s to the mid-1940s Bahraini society remained relatively stable. The Al Khalifah occupied a predominant position within the country's political and economic affairs, supported not only by the growing amounts of petroleum revenues coming into the central government's coffers but also by the corps of British advisers attached to the imperial administration. Local merchant families that had lost their primary source of wealth with the collapse of the pearling industry, following the development of cultured pearls by the Japanese, attempted to maintain their fortunes through a variety of new activities: some by selling off family-held land and other forms of real estate; some by providing foodstuffs, lumber, and other supplies to the oil company at Awali and the British military bases on the islands; others by lending funds to more impoverished traders and budding entrepreneurs; and still others by entering into exclusive marketing agreements with foreign firms operating in the Gulf. As these ventures began to prosper, Bahrain's commercial elite regained some degree of influence over the country's internal affairs.

But in the years during and immediately following World War II, three interrelated developments gradually undermined the imperial order on the islands. In the first place, Bahrain's central administration extended its supervision over a wide range of economic and social affairs within the country, introducing an unprecedented degree of state control over the operations of private commercial and industrial enterprises. Second, the expansion of foreign firms into the Gulf provided a growing number of opportunities for the more prestigious and better-connected merchant houses to consolidate their hold over Bahrain's foreign trading sector, thereby improving their position relative to that of the ruling family. Finally, the rise of a considerable class of nouveaux riches traders within the local economy, composed primarily of South Asian expatriates whose

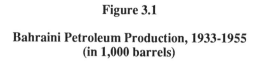

Figure 3.1

Bahraini Petroleum Production, 1933-1955
(in 1,000 barrels)

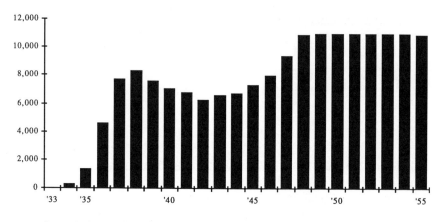

Source: Mohammed Ghanim al-Rumaihi, *Bahrain: A Study on Social and Political*
Changes Since the First World War (Kuwait: Kuwait University
Press, 1975), p. 99; George Lenczowski, *Oil and State in the Middle*
East (Ithaca: Cornell University Press, 1960), p. 361; Keith McLachlan,
"Oil in the Persian Gulf Area," in Alvin J. Cottrell, ed., *The Persian*
Gulf States (Baltimore: Johns Hopkins University Press, 1980),
pp. 212-213. Al-Rumaihi reports a substantially lower figure for 1955
(9,196,500 tons) than does any other authority; the figure included here
(10,950,000 tons) reflects the general consensus.

presence on the islands was sanctioned if not actively encouraged by
the British authorities, created a serious challenge to the virtually
monopolistic position that the indigenous rich merchant community had
previously occupied in Bahraini markets. The interplay of these three
dynamics provided the basis for the liberal nationalist movement that
emerged within the country during the early 1950s, a movement whose
limited successes left the regime vulnerable to more radical opponents
by the middle of the decade.

ECONOMIC CHANGE AND POLITICAL ADAPTATION

Bahrain provided an almost paradigmatic case of peaceful political
accommodation to profound economic transformation during the decade
following the consolidation of the imperial regime on the islands in the
early 1930s. Petroleum production increased dramatically after 1935,
leveling off at around 1 million tons (1.016 million metric tons) per year
for the 1937–1940 period (see Figure 3.1). Revenues from this sector of

TABLE 3.1
Revenues from Petroleum Production, 1934/35-1955

	Rupees (1,000)	Proportion of Total Revenues (percent)
1934/35	379	32.9
1935/36	461	32.6
1936/37	2,110	64.3
1937/38	2,363	66.3
1938/39	2,157	61.6
1939/40	2,368	63.7
1940/41	1,977	57.4
1941/42	1,748	56.2
1942/43	1,807	47.6
1943/44	1,859	40.6
1944/45	2,017	37.4
1945/46	2,073	36.8
1946/47	2,601	35.2
1947/48	3,061	34.8
1948/49	3,281	31.1
1949/50	6,255	45.1
1950/51	10,226	51.0
1951/52	13,401	53.1
1952/53	27,656	61.4
1954	35,002	71.1
1955	28,370	63.8

Source: Mohammed Ghanim al-Rumaihi, *Bahrain: A Study on Social and Political Changes Since the First World War* (Kuwait: Kuwait University Press, 1975), p. 105.

the economy, which had provided about one-third of the state's total budget in the mid-1930s, contributed between 60 percent and 65 percent of the government's income in the five years prior to 1940 (see Table 3.1). At the same time, such central economic activities as boat construction and date palm agriculture declined precipitously, leaving considerable numbers of poorer villagers out of work. The impact of these dislocations was somewhat less severe in the northern and eastern coastal districts, where fishing continued to provide employment and food for the local population. Bahraini commerce remained largely unaffected by these shifts in the country's economic affairs; this trade continued to consist for the most part of such staples as rice, tea, wheat, sugar, meat, and cloth, the greatest share of which was reexported to Saudi Arabia.

These economic changes had little if any effect on the structure of Bahraini politics. Shaikh Hamad's program of using oil revenues to rationalize the country's central administration effectively removed a number of potential sources of discontent with Al Khalifah rule as the 1930s went by. By replacing the semiofficial pearling tribunals with government courts and implementing stricter regulations on working conditions within the pearling industry, the imperial regime was able to prevent the richer merchants and their agents from undermining the reforms of 1932–1933. As a result, the number of vessels taking part in the annual pearl expeditions gradually rose in the years just before World War II. In the oil field at Awali, close cooperation among the ruler's advisers, the British authorities, and Bahrain Petroleum Company's on-site supervisors kept workers' grievances to a minimum. Lieutenant-Colonel P. G. Loch, the Political Agent in Bahrain during the late 1930s, describes the administration of petroleum affairs on the islands in the following words:

> As you can imagine, things were not always easy—for example, the question arose of compensation for accidents, and really our only guide was the blood-feud. Well, we came to the conclusion that a basis of litigation or even of blood-feud would be hopeless, so gradually there grew up an informal board of the Political Agent and Assistant Political Agent, the Adviser to the Bahrain Government, and the Chief Local Representative and the Field Manager of the Company. We used to meet as soon after any serious accident as we could get definite medical information about the extent of the injury. . . . Payment was then made forthwith through the Bahrain Government. We never had any disagreement, and I do not think that the awards were ever questioned.[1]

Moreover, the ruler appropriated funds to train and equip a camel-mounted police force charged with enforcing a modicum of law and order among the predominantly tribal populations of outlying districts. This force succeeded not only in regulating the flow of arms across Bahrain's borders but also in cementing ties between the Al Khalifah and the country's other more influential clans.

As the 1930s drew to a close, two developments threatened to upset the equilibrium of Bahrain's imperial order. In the first place, considerable numbers of South Asian workers migrated into the country as oil production expanded during the latter half of the decade. This migration was encouraged by the British authorities, who were interested in replacing the Persian work force at the Bahrain Petroleum Company (BAPCO) with skilled Indian labor in an effort to undercut Iran's claim to sovereignty over the archipelago. The residency staff stepped up its drive to recruit Indian workers after the police carried out a series of deportations of Persian "illegal immigrants" in 1937–1938.[2] But this effort met with continuous resistance from the management of the oil company, for whom southern Iran constituted a considerably cheaper and more accessible source of skilled labor than did the subcontinent. Consequently, the number of Persian workers on the islands remained quite large during the early years of the war.

Second, the steady deterioration of local agricultural production heightened the importance of imported foodstuffs within the Bahraini market. By the late 1930s, the greatest part of the wheat, rice, and tea consumed on the islands was being imported from India; most of the country's sugar came from East Africa; and dates for human use were brought in from Iraq and Saudi Arabia, whereas those for livestock continued to be grown locally. The increasing role of imports in the country's economy enhanced the position of Bahrain's merchant community relative to that of the ruling family and its British advisers. The growing influence of the richer merchants in domestic affairs was acknowledged by the imperial regime in 1939, when a chamber of commerce made up of the most respected members of the country's commercial establishment was formed in Manama.

THE IMPACT OF WORLD WAR II

With the coming of World War II, the regime subjected both the Persian expatriate community on the islands and the larger foreign trading houses to greater administrative control in the name of national security. In early July 1941, just prior to the joint British-Soviet invasion of Iran, government officials rounded up approximately 150 of Bahrain's Persian residents and expelled those whose papers were not in order. A year before this move, the government had extended its hold over the country's food supply by purchasing 25,000 bags of Indian rice to be used as a state-controlled reserve, banning any export of foodstuffs and ordering local merchants to provide state officials with complete inventories of their goods on hand.[3] The first rationing of staples took place in March 1942, when the district administration for Manama set up eight outlets for distributing sugar. Price controls on a wide range of other imported items were introduced at about the same time. During the first months of 1943, as dates came to be in short supply throughout the country, government officials negotiated with Iraq and Saudi Arabia for emergency shipments of both date pulses and date stones (used as feed for livestock). These consignments were distributed at police stations in the outlying villages. Three state-run food stores opened in Manama later that same year. By mid-1944 Bahrain's central administration had taken charge of virtually all of the rice, sugar, dates, flour, tea, and meat sold on local markets.

As government agencies became more involved in domestic economic affairs, local merchants acted to circumvent the wartime restrictions on Bahrain's foreign trade. Sugar and other imported foodstuffs were continually smuggled out of the country during the first years of the war. Unauthorized shipments of building materials and spare parts to Iraq and eastern Arabia increased substantially after about 1942. These activities became more profitable as trading relations with India were subjected to more frequent interruptions; in early 1944 the British Political Agent reported that "no general cargo had been received for 11½ weeks— what ships did arrive merely brought cement for the airfield."[4] As a result, pilfering at both BAPCO and the military air base proliferated, producing a sharp increase in the number of cases of theft brought before the criminal court.

State officials responded to the growing incidence of both smuggling and hoarding of scarce goods by creating a merchants' advisory committee charged with overseeing trading practices on the islands. The body met intermittently throughout the war but adopted no program of action to deal with illicit operations on the part of its constituents. Government agents then resorted to confiscating the stocks of convicted black marketeers. But even this tactic failed to prevent substantial fortunes from being made during the course of the war through the workings of the country's black market.

Wartime shortages combined with the evident success of local import-export merchants in turning these shortages to their own advantage created considerable discontent among the poorer agricultural and industrial laborers on the islands. Strict wage controls imposed during the first months of the war kept salaries in the oil sector depressed relative both to those in local commerce and services and to those in neighboring countries. As demand for both skilled and unskilled labor rose in early 1943, with the successive decisions on the part of the Royal Air Force to enlarge the airfield at Muharraq and by BAPCO to enlarge and modernize the refinery at Sitra, opposition to the low wages permitted by the government grew.

This opposition finally precipitated a walkout by Bahraini refinery workers in mid-December 1943; the company's transportation and dock workers immediately followed suit.[5] After local officials failed in their attempt to mediate the dispute, BAPCO offered the striking workers additional benefits and a supplementary War Allowance on condition that they return to work by the end of the month. At the same time, the police put the alleged leaders of the strike under arrest. Faced with this carrot and stick, virtually all of the strikers returned to their jobs before the deadline. State officials reacted to the evident strength of the labor movement by setting up a labor committee made up of representatives of the islands' main employers and the armed forces. In addition, the imperial administration brought a company of Indian soldiers to the refinery complex the following summer to work in the newly opened aviation fuel facility.

By the time the war ended, Bahrain's central administration had extended its control over a wide range of commercial and industrial operations on the islands. The expansion of the state may be inferred from the rise in government revenues that occurred during this period: In 1939–1940 these had amounted to a little more than 3.7 million rupees ($1.5 million) (almost 64 percent of which came from oil); six years later they had reached more than 5.6 million rupees ($2.26 million) (of which only about 37 percent came from oil).[6] More important, state officials took on a major role in supervising the construction and management of modern manufacturing plants, as well as in regulating workers' affairs. These moves were supplemented by the government's growing involvement in the areas of health care and education. In 1942 the state hospital was enlarged, and a network of dispensaries was extended to include most of the larger villages; between 1940 and 1945 Manama College for young men and two additional schools for girls were opened in the capital. These developments made the state the dominant component of the country's ruling coalition during the late 1940s. Not until the labor unrest of 1947–1948, in the course of which government officials lifted the wartime restrictions on the emigration of Bahraini labor and BAPCO regained control over industrial relations within the country, did this political configuration begin to change.

THE EXPANSION OF FOREIGN FIRMS

Throughout the 1940s, international corporations based in Great Britain and the United States moved into the Gulf region in an effort to tap potential markets for construction equipment and consumer goods in the more prosperous oil-producing areas. These corporations had met with little success in dealing with eastern Arabia through wholly-owned subsidiaries over the previous decade and so began to establish exclusive marketing arrangements with local merchant families. By collecting the rights to import and distribute Western products in regional markets, a small number of prominent commercial houses not only amassed considerable fortunes but also reestablished themselves in powerful positions within their respective societies. In the case of Bahrain, this process can be illustrated through the stories of three business families whose members used their contacts to outside concerns to recover the losses they had suffered in the collapse of the pearling industry and subsequent depression of the 1930s.[7]

Yusuf al-Mu'ayyid left his family's pearl business in the late 1930s and set himself up as a small-scale iron goods trader in Manama. Over the next few years he learned English and developed amicable relationships with both the quartermaster at the RAF airfield outside Muharraq and the local representatives of Imperial Airways, whose aircraft touched down at the airfield on their journey between Iraq to the west and Sharjah and Karachi to the east. As activity at the airfield accelerated during the war, al-Mu'ayyid acted as middleperson between the British garrision and the local bazaar, obtaining a commission of 5 percent on the goods he supplied to the base. His reputation among the military supply personnel became established when he returned a check for 3,000 rupees ($1,200) that the air force had mistakenly issued twice; such honesty encouraged the RAF to make greater use of his services, and by 1945 his fortune had reached almost £50,000 ($210,000). In addition, immediately after the war the RAF provided him with a free trip to London, from which he returned with exclusive rights to market General Electric products on the islands. Al-Mu'ayyid traveled to the United States in 1948 and negotiated an agency arrangement with General Motors on similar terms. His wartime contacts enabled his firm to establish close working relationships with a wide range of other firms in the Gulf, including British Overseas Aircraft Corporation (BOAC) and Cable and Wireless.

A parallel course was taken by Ahmad and Muhammad Kanu, the grand-nephews of Yusuf bin Ahmad Kanu. By the late 1940s, the family's firm—which consisted of the local agencies for four different shipping lines, for the Anglo-Iranian Oil Company, and for Nash automobiles— had fallen on hard times. In an effort to improve the company's competitiveness relative to the British firm Gray Mackenzie, the brothers undertook a series of trips abroad to visit the home offices of the more important trading companies bringing imported goods into the islands. Several of these companies, no doubt impressed by the straightforward approach to business adopted by the Kanus, agreed to off-load future cargoes on the Kanus' barges rather than on those operated by their British rival. These contracts were followed by agreements with the British underwriters Norwich Union and BOAC to set up branch offices for selling insurance and airline tickets, respectively, on the islands.

Perhaps the greatest coup carried off by the Kanus occurred in 1951. Ahmad and Muhammad used their long-standing contacts with overseas shipping lines and with the commander of the U.S. naval station at Jufair to gain a virtual monopoly on tanker operations involving both the outlet of the Arabian-American Oil Company (ARAMCO) at Dammam and shipments of Gulf-produced gasoline and aviation fuel to the U.S. Military Sea Transportation Services. These moves put the Kanus in a position to draw new customers coming into the Gulf after 1950 away from Gray Mackenzie, whose administrative procedures they increasingly duplicated.

Husain Yatim augmented his family's fortune in a more entrepreneurial fashion. Favorably impressed by the British aviator Freddie Bosworth, who arrived at Muharraq in a disintegrating Anson Mark I aircraft in April 1942, he lent the pilot 2,000 rupees ($800) to buy spare parts from the ARAMCO supply center at Dhahran. Eight years later Yatim provided the capital for the creation of the Gulf Aviation Company Limited. Upon the death of Bosworth, he negotiated an arrangement with BOAC whereby the latter would operate regular flights joining Muharraq to Dhahran and Sharjah under Gulf Aviation's auspices. By the early 1950s, the firm Yatim Brothers had used the profits from its original investment in Gulf Aviation to expand into a variety of import-export businesses.

By means such as these, Bahrain's rich merchant community created a commercial boom on the islands in the years immediately after World War II. Precise figures that might document this trend are unavailable, but more impressionistic evidence indicates that imports flowed into the country in unprecedented quantitites during this period. In November 1948, a visiting reporter remarked that Manama's "well-stocked bazaar is a relief to Aramco wives who have tired of the limited wares available in Dhahran's glorified PX."[8] James Belgrave observed some two years later that "the shops in the main towns of Bahrain are improving in appearance and contents: they are full of British and American goods, necessities and luxuries, such as tinned foods, radios, and cameras, which were at first imported for the use of the Europeans and rich Arabs, but are now to be found in many middle-class Arab houses."[9] In addition to providing goods for the domestic market, Bahraini merchants handled substantial quantities of imported manufactured goods destined for Qatar and the Trucial States. Foreign firms exploring for oil in these relatively remote areas purchased virtually all of their equipment from agents in Manama during the late 1940s and early 1950s. As a result of this upsurge in foreign trade, the proportion of government revenues derived from customs duties rose continuously from 1945 to 1949, reducing petroleum revenues to an all-time low of 31 percent of total state income in fiscal year 1948/49.

THE RISE OF THE NOUVEAUX RICHES

Increasing levels of activity in Bahrain's foreign and domestic trading sectors provided a wide range of opportunities for small-scale tradespeople within the local economy as the 1950s began. Despite the growing influence of the richer merchant houses, the great majority of commercial and industrial enterprises continued to be composed of smaller stores and workshops. The 1956 industrial census for the islands lists 2,507 trading and banking concerns, the average size of which was only 2.3 persons. Among the 687 manufacturing establishments included in this census, more than half were single-person operations, and the average employment in this sector stood at a mere 2.5 persons.[10] These firms were able to adapt quickly and efficiently to shifts in demand within the indigenous market, enabling their owners to prosper during the boom conditions of the late 1940s.

What was most striking to outside observers about the smaller commercial and industrial enterprises that proliferated on the islands after the war was the predominance of foreign nationals running them. In April 1949 Belgrave reported that there were 215 Indian-owned shops in the Manama bazaar alone; during the next few years non-Bahrainis became the owners of a majority of the country's factories and work-shops.[11] Under these circumstances, the established pattern of labor relations—in which Westerners occupied the management positions, South Asians the middle-level ones, and poorer native Bahrainis the entry-level clerical and manual slots—was accentuated, leading to growing popular discontent over the number of foreigners employed by local companies.

But foreign nationals were not the only tradespeople whose social position improved around 1950. A variety of Shi'i and nonelite Sunni traders moved into the top ranks of the local economic hierarchy during these years as well. The merchant houses of Mirza Hussain Khoshabi, Muhammad Tayyib Khonji, and the Behbehanis, which handled a wide range of imported manufactured goods, offered serious competition to the country's established commercial firms at this time, not just on local markets but in other parts of the Gulf as well. These interests gradually demanded a level of representation on Bahrain's governing councils commensurate with their new economic standing in the community. After a series of appeals to the imperial authorities, the nouveaux riches merchants finally had their demands acknowledged in early 1951, when the government reorganized the structure of the Chamber of Commerce to include greater participation by middle-level and small-scale traders operating on the islands.

The growing prosperity of the smaller Sunni and Shi'i traders was reflected in the proliferation of cultural societies and mourning houses that took place in the towns and villages of Bahrain during the years just after the war. Most of the larger cultural societies had been founded in the late 1930s: Nadi al-Bahrain based in Muharraq grew out of the

Shops in the Manama *suq* circa 1950. Source: Charles Belgrave, *Personal Column* (London: Hutchinson, 1960), facing p. 93.

older ash-Shabibah soccer club in 1937; Manama-based Sunni merchants formed the al-Ahli club a year later; prominent Shi'i merchants and government employees established Nadi al-'Uruba in 1939. But these associations flourished during the postwar period, attracting new members from among the country's smaller tradespeople, secondary-school students, teachers, government employees, and skilled workers.[12]

Club members met regularly to discuss both local and regional affairs, a development perceived by the British authorities as contributing to the growth of "political consciousness" among "educated young men."[13] Nadi al-Bahrain and Nadi al-'Uruba emerged as centers of Arab nationalist sentiment during the late 1940s. Richer Persian merchants responded to the spread of more popular societies by establishing the Firdawsi cultural and sports club in 1946 to channel upwardly mobile young Shi'is into less politically charged pursuits; four years earlier the Al Khalifah had set up the Islah association among proregime forces in Muharraq for much the same purpose. Because of their evident connections to the islands' political and economic establishment, these latter societies were unable to attract much of a following among nonelite Bahrainis.

Within the country's Shi'i community a parallel development involved the mourning houses (*matam*) responsible for organizing the annual commemoration of the martyrdom of the Imam Husain, known as 'Ashura.[14] Prior to the 1940s, the most prominent of these houses were to be found in Manama. They had been constructed during the decades around the turn of the twentieth century by richer Shi'i merchants as a way of enhancing their families' prestige in local society. As the original benefactors began to die off in the mid-1940s, most of these houses fell under the control of informal associations of prominent urban traders having close ties to the state-affiliated administration for endowments (*awqaf*). This trend reinforced the position of the country's Shi'i commercial and religious oligarchy relative to that of the nouveaux riches and led the latter to set up "family-organized, faction-oriented houses" in the outlying towns and villages as alternatives to the "association-based houses" in the larger cities. By the mid-1950s virtually all of Bahrain's smaller communities contained at least one independent mourning house and many villages had more than one. The newer houses served not only as symbols of the rising importance of the younger Shi'i tradespeople but also as legitimate fora in which political grievances against the regime could be aired and opposition to the authorities mobilized.

ORIGINS OF THE LIBERAL NATIONALIST MOVEMENT

Two fundamental shifts in Bahraini politics during the early 1950s laid the groundwork for the rise of a liberal nationalist movement on the islands. On the one hand, government officials made a concerted effort to reestablish state control over the country's commercial affairs by revising the system of customs duties levied on goods coming into and out of Bahrain's ports. This move was buttressed by a substantial increase in petroleum revenues accruing to the treasury after 1950. And it was furthered by the disruption in Gulf trade occasioned by Britain's attempts to destabilize the Mossadegh regime in Iran and Saudi Arabia's efforts to expand the port at Dammam. On the other hand, changes in hiring patterns at BAPCO installations, combined with increasing emigration of skilled Bahraini labor and a consequent rise in the number of South Asian workers entering the country, precipitated violent clashes between poorer forces remaining on the islands competing for access to better-paying industrial and construction jobs. The conjunction of these two trends led more moderate representatives of the nouveaux riches to advocate wide-ranging reforms in the imperial order as a way of reducing the potential for sectarian conflict on the islands.

As Bahrain's foreign trade continued to prosper after 1948, state officials began to reconsider the minimal customs duties levied on imports coming into the local market. These duties had been set at 2 percent of total value in the late 1920s, when King 'Abd al-'Aziz Al Saud had prevailed upon the Political Agent to lower the duty on goods passing through Bahraini harbors on their way to ports on the mainland. Consequently, the government found itself at a severe disadvantage relative to private commercial interests when both imports and reexports surged in the immediate postwar period. In an effort to improve its position with regard to the country's foreign trading sector, the central administration issued a revised customs ordinance in January 1950 that raised the basic tariff on goods coming into the islands to 5 percent ad valorem. This duty applied to all foodstuffs and other basic imported commodities handled by local trading houses. On a number of luxury items, however, the duty was increased to 10 percent, whereas goods destined for the royal family and BAPCO were exempted from all tariffs. Export duties were assessed on an item-by-item basis, but these charges for the most part remained around 2 percent. As a result of these changes in the customs, nonoil income to the state budget rose by 21.8 percent in fiscal year 1950/51 and by an additional 45.6 percent the following year.

At the same time that the state was receiving greater revenues from foreign trade, changes in the rate of royalty payments on Bahrain's oil concession increased government income from this sector of the economy as well. Prior to 1950, annual royalty payments by BAPCO to the central treasury averaged about £400,000 ($1.6 million); for 1950/51 they rose to around £1 million ($2.8 million), and beginning in 1952 they reached almost £2.25 million ($6.3 million). These increases resulted from an agreement concluded in 1950 setting the rate of payment by the company at 10.2 rupees per metric ton (10 rupees per long ton), up from the earlier level of 3.06 rupees per metric ton (3 rupees per long ton), and from the adoption of a variable-rate income tax on company operations effective as of January 1952 that introduced the principle of 50 percent profit-sharing already in place in the other Gulf oil-producing countries.[15] The primary beneficiary of these measures was the Al Khalifah, whose members saw their share of BAPCO revenues jump from around $1.5 million in 1949 to $3.3 million in 1950 and then to $6.3 million in 1952.

Meanwhile, both the established commercial elite and the nouveaux riches traders on the islands were affected by dislocations in regional trade resulting from developments on the northern and western shores of the Gulf. To the north, Bahrain's extensive reexport trade with southern Iran suffered as Great Britain stepped up its efforts to cut the nationalist regime led by Dr. Mohammad Mossadegh off from the outside world. In September 1951, the British treasury revoked the arrangement whereby Iran was allowed to convert pounds Sterling into U.S. dollars to pay for imports and announced that all future transactions in Sterling would be subject to its approval; at the same time, the British authorities withdrew Tehran's privileged access to certain goods considered scarce and regulated by export controls. These moves almost immediately reduced the flow of U.S. and British trade coming into the Gulf region by way of Bahraini ports. To the west, the expansion of the Saudi port at Dammam diverted a large proportion of the cloth, lumber, machinery, and foodstuffs bound for the kingdom's eastern province away from Bahraini harbors. Furthermore, in a move designed to discourage private individuals from undermining its program of developing Dammam, the Saudi government imposed a substantial tax on anyone traveling to Bahrain to shop.[16]

These developments had a particularly serious impact on the Hawala merchant community of Manama, whose fortunes were most closely connected to the trade with areas along the Gulf littoral. The members of this community responded to the commercial dislocations of the early 1950s by criticizing BAPCO for its long-standing practice of importing materials used at the refinery and drilling areas directly rather than through local trading houses. At the same time, commercial interests expressed growing discontent with the operation of the country's judicial system, the civil branch of which was dominated by largely unqualified shaikhs from the Al Khalifah.[17] Much of this disconent was directed at the resident Indian trading community, in whose favor the courts were alleged to be biased in their deliberations. By 1952, leading representatives of Nadi al-Bahrain, Nadi al-'Uruba, and the al-Ahli Club had formed a network of Arab nationalist activists opposed to the British presence on the islands and the predominance of the ruling family within the regime. This grouping was made up of both Sunnis and Shi'a, many of whom had participated in the 1938 reform movement.

Opposition to the regime began to smolder among Bahrain's in-dustrial proletariat by the early 1950s as well. Activity at BAPCO facilities around Sitra had increased sharply in the years after 1948 with the installation of an asphalt plant, the enlargement of the drum factory and its associated filling station, and the continual expansion of the refinery itself. These operations led the company to increase the size of its total staff from 6,078 to 7,749 in early 1951. As a result of the emigration of skilled Bahraini laborers to other, higher-paying parts of the Gulf, the number of indigenous employees rose by only 287 persons, reducing the proportion of native workers at BAPCO from 76 percent to 64 percent.[18] These workers were concentrated in the ranks of the company's noncontract or daily wage-rate labor force, whereas South Asian workers remained predominant within the contract or monthly-paid ranks. As a result, working-class Bahrainis became increasingly disaffected with both the oil company, whose management appeared oblivious to local sensitivities, and the imperial administration, under whose auspices South Asian immigrants entered the islands. Moreover, the rising level of competition for better-paying jobs in the petroleum sector generated a growing amount of tension among disadvantaged groups within the country. This tension erupted into violence on a variety of occasions between 1952 and 1954.

Aside from the relatively diffuse industrial unrest of early 1947, which had been largely rooted in an attempt by Indian workers at BAPCO to create a committee to express their grievances, political disorder had first occurred on the islands during the winter of 1947–1948, in response to the United Nations plan to partition Palestine into a Jewish zone and an Arab zone. This proposal precipitated a riot in Muharraq directed against U.S. and Soviet support for the plan; but the demonstration soon transformed itself into a protest against all foreign interests, particularly the oil company. The leaders of this movement organized themselves into a National Front and published broadsheets urging workers, merchants, clerics, and other indigenous forces to unite in a "patriotic struggle" for independence.[19] The movement failed to win widespread support and soon dissipated in the general economic upswing of the late 1940s.

By the time the postwar boom ended, working-class disorder had begun to take on a pronounced sectarian cast. At the end of 1952, rioting broke out in the poorer sections of Manama over the issue of representation among Sunnis and Shi'a on the municipal council. During the commemoration of 'Ashura in September 1953, fighting occurred between Shi'i mourners and Sunni onlookers at a ritual procession in the al-Fadil section of Manama. This incident prompted a subsequent attack by a Sunni mob on a Shi'i village on Muharraq Island, as well as a number of other skirmishes in outlying districts. The following June, Shi'i and Sunni workers clashed outside the refinery complex at Sitra. When the Shi'i community concluded that its members arrested during the fighting had been treated unfairly by the courts, a crowd formed in the mosque directly across from the jail and attempted to release their coreligionists by storm. Guards opened fire on the mob, killing four of the attackers.

In the wake of this incident, Bahrain's nouveaux riches traders undertook to redirect sectarian conflict on the islands into less divisive, and therefore more manageable, channels. Shopkeepers in Manama initiated a week-long general strike in mid-July to protest the actions of the police. More significantly, the network of Arab nationalist activists appealed to notables within each of the two communities to cooperate with one another in bringing Sunni-Shi'a clashes to an end.[20] When the country's bus and taxi drivers struck in September to demonstrate their opposition to the government's plan to insure their vehicles through foreign-owned companies, this network proposed to settle the dispute by setting up a locally controlled cooperative compensation bureau administered by prominent merchants and vehicle operators. The proposal was accepted by all parties concerned, heightening the prestige of the network and setting the stage for a public rally in support of 'Abd al-'Aziz Shamlan, 'Abd ar-Rahman al-Bakir, and other nationalist leaders.

This rally—convened at al-Khamis mosque, the only one on the islands respected by both Sunnis and Shi'a—led to another in Sanabis on 13 October at which 120 representatives were elected to a nascent national assembly. The representatives then nominated eight members to a Higher Executive Committee (HEC) consisting of four Sunnis and four Shi'is. Of the Sunnis, three were Arab nationalists from Muharraq and one was a merchant from al-Hidd; of the Shi'a, one was a merchant, one was a cleric, one organized 'Ashura processions, and one was a worker at BAPCO.[21] The formation of the HEC marked a high point in intercommunal cooperation, tarnished only by the establishment of a separate national committee by Manama's Hawala merchants.

Immediately after its formation, the HEC published a list of reforms it expected the regime to implement. These included the creation of an elected legislative council, the adoption of a codified system of criminal and civil laws, the establishment of trade unions and the appointment of a court of appeals. The HEC argued that such measures were necessary if public unrest were to be brought to an end and the country's administrative structure made adequate to deal with the problems of the modern age. In an open letter to the amir, the committee assured Shaikh Sulman that "these demands do not aim to interfere with the position of the Ruler and do not conflict with the interests of the British Government."[22] It then appointed a delegation to present these proposals to the ruler formally. When the amir refused to receive the delegation, the HEC declared a week-long general strike and made clandestine overtures to the British authorities.

THE APOGEE OF LIBERAL NATIONALISM

During October and November of 1954, the HEC organized two major public rallies in Manama, one at the Shi'i Mu'min mosque and one at the Sunni al-'Id mosque. These meetings were held on major festival days—commemorating the fortieth day after the martyrdom of the Imam Husain and the birthday of the Prophet Muhammad, respectively—and drew approximately 10,000 participants each from all parts of the country. Cowed by this unprecedented demonstration of

popular support, the regime initiated secret talks with HEC representatives. These discussions soon collapsed, however, as the ruler would
not countenance the principle of election as a legitimate basis for authority.
The nationalists responded by calling a peaceful general strike for the
week beginning 4 December. This strike succeeded in bringing commercial
and industrial activity on the islands to a standstill, prompting the amir
to decree that a committee would be created to oversee education,
health, and police matters, and elections would be held for a new
municipal council. In the end, the HEC rejected the proposed services
committee on the grounds that it included disproportionate representation
from the Al Khalifah and its allies and failed to put forward the requisite
number of candidates for the municipal elections. But the HEC achieved
two notable successes during the months between July 1955 and March
1956: It drew up plans to establish a general trades union organization,
and it gained official recognition as an independent political organization.

During the summer of 1955, the regime announced its intention
to set up an advisory committee to draft a proposed labor law, and
BAPCO made public its plans to establish consultative committees made
up of representatives of both management and labor at its various plants.
The HEC responded to these initiatives by declaring that it planned to
form a labor federation of its own under the leadership of Muhammad
ash-Shirawi. Offices for this federation were opened in a number of
poorer districts of Manama; by the end of October some 6,000 workers
had become dues-paying members of the organization.[23] The following
February a constituent committee met to determine what sort of structure
the labor federation would have and how its directors would be elected.
As a result of this body's deliberations, the federation was set up as a
single overarching trade union organization governed by a 16-member
administrative council and an 84-member general assembly. In addition,
the federation reserved for itself the right to appoint any workers'
representatives to company-mandated joint consultative committees. Elections to both the administrative council and the general assembly were
set for the fall of 1956. On the whole, the HEC's efforts at creating such
a labor organization presented the regime with a fait accompli that
succeeded in undermining the more marginal reforms formulated by
state and BAPCO officials.

Official recognition of the HEC as a legitimate actor in Bahraini
politics was more difficult to gain. The first act in this drama occurred
in February 1956, when the committee's leadership agreed to participate
in elections for representatives to the state-sponsored education council.
HEC candidates won more than 90 percent of the vote in this election,
only to have their victory undercut by the appointment to the council
of two regime-sponsored candidates who had been defeated at the polls.

In protest against this move, the HEC delegates refused to take part in the council's deliberations until the two members were removed. The imperial authorities eventually relented on this issue, but appointed the amir's uncle, Shaikh 'Abdullah bin 'Isa, as permanent head of the council, prompting the HEC to continue their boycott.

The next act took place the following month with a series of meetings between the British Political Agent and leaders of the committee. In the course of these meetings, the Agent worked out a compromise whereby the HEC would drop its long-standing demands for the creation of an elected legislative council and the dismissal of the ruler's adviser in exchange for government recognition, with the proviso that the committee change its name as a way of disassociating itself from the regime's more radical opponents. The leaders of the HEC agreed to this proposal on 17 March. The following day, al-Bakir, ash-Shamlan, and other prominent nationalists witnessed the amir's signing of a decree recognizing a Committee of National Unity (CNU) as a legal entity.

Two days later, the ruler proclaimed the formation of an administrative council headed by Shaikh 'Abdullah. The members of this council included three other senior members of the Al Khalifah, G.W.R. Smith (the former head of the customs department), and three of the islands' leading merchants. This body was authorized "to arrange matters between government departments in order to improve their functions, to contact the people and to carry out the amir's orders." It was prohibited from interferring "with the State's finances, nor with political or foreign affairs."[24] The CNU immediately attacked this body on the grounds that its members were appointed rather than elected and that its powers were too narrowly circumscribed. In a bulletin issued in July, the committee urged the general public to reject the council and continue its support for the CNU's program of working to establish trades unions, a free press, improved systems of health care and education, and a diversified industrial base on the islands. Persistent pressure on the part of the committee led the government to announce in mid-August that its British adviser would retire the following summer. But the ouster of Belgrave represented the denouement of the CNU's battle to limit the powers of the Al Khalifah and reform the country's administrative apparatus. Other, more radical forces had taken the initiative in the anticolonial struggle by the spring of 1956.

THE RADICAL CHALLENGE

The liberal nationalists' success in forcing the regime to adopt political and social reforms encouraged a variety of less moderate forces within Bahraini society to challenge the established order as well. Within the Shi'i community, for example, the mid-1950s saw the establishment of the Ja'fari League, an organization of students and lower-level state employees in the suburb of Jidd Hafs committed to eliminating illiteracy and promoting unity among their coreligionists. The activities of this organization gradually weakened the position of the Shi'i religious establishment and created the potential for grass-roots political action on the part of poorer Shi'is in the countryside. More significantly, the HEC's criticism of the British imperial administration precipitated two outbreaks of violent political disorder that signaled the growing inability of the moderates to control the course of antiregime activity on the islands.

On 2 March 1956 Britain's foreign minister, Selwyn Lloyd, made a brief stop in Bahrain on his way to East Asia. While proceeding from the airfield outside Muharraq to the government palace in Manama, his motorcade passed a crowd of spectators leaving a soccer match. The crowd began chanting slogans attacking the ruler, his British adviser, and British imperialism in general; it soon grew into a mob and began throwing rocks not only at the cars of the visiting dignitaries but also at the ruler's Rolls-Royce. Police dispersed the rioters after two hours and the HEC publicly condemned their actions the following day. But spontaneous disturbances continued throughout the country over the next week, culminating in a much more serious incident on 11 March.

That day a Shi'i trader set up a stall in the Manama bazaar without permission from the district inspector. The events that ensued are summarized by Fuad Khuri:

> The inspector called the police, who arrested the peddler and drove him to the municipal building at the entrance of the marketplace. Soon a large crowd of sympathizers and fellow "villagers" gathered around the municipal building and besieged a group of policemen. Two parties of policemen were ordered to move out from the fort, at the other end of the city, and rescue their colleagues at the municipal building. One party reached the building, but the other was held by an angry crowd some distance away. To disperse the crowd, some policemen inside the building opened fire and killed five persons. Succumbing to pressure, particularly from the Shi'a representatives on the HEC, the committee immediately declared a general stike that lasted several days.[25]

This strike was not as peaceful as earlier ones had been: Small bands of protesters set up roadblocks and damaged private automobiles of those who ignored the work stoppage. Militants within the HEC organization began forming "first-aid teams" to supervise these actions and keep them focused on political goals. By the early summer of 1956, government officials were charging that the radical wing of the CNU was smuggling weapons into the country from southern Iran. These charges gained credibility in June when, in response to the regime's decision to prosecute none of the police officers involved in the killings of early March, the committee set up a paramilitary force of uniformed activists called the "scouts."[26]

In the wake of the British-French-Israeli invasion of Egypt later that fall, moderates within the CNU lost virtually all control over the committee's more radical supporters. Students at the country's secondary schools demonstrated in Manama and Muharraq on 30–31 October, chanting anti-British and anti-Israeli slogans and setting fire to private automobiles and foreign-owned businesses. A mass rally in Manama on 2 November quickly turned into a riot in the course of which the local offices of Gray Mackenzie, a number of houses of British expatriates in Muharraq and a filling station belonging to BAPCO were set afire. Buildings housing government agencies and British commercial firms were also attacked and looted. The following day rioters severely damaged the barges and loading equipment of Gray Mackenzie in Manama harbor and attempted to burn down the offices of the public works department. In response to these events, the regime declared a state of emergency and ordered police units—reinforced by British troops deployed to Bahrain in March—to arrest al-Bakir, ash-Shamlan, and their colleagues.

THE SUPPRESSION OF
THE NATIONALIST MOVEMENTS

Bahrain's imperial regime used a variety of means to suppress its radical opponents during the last quarter of 1956. Most obvious was the government's reliance upon its police forces to break up anti-regime demonstrations, whereby it took advantage of the expansion and modernization of these units carried out by the central administration throughout the mid-1950s. In addition, the ruling coalition maintained the support of the country's tribal population, whose members' political and economic position improved as a result of the programs adopted by the regime during the nationalist period. Finally, shifts in purchasing policies at BAPCO neutralized a good deal of potential opposition to the dominant coalition by increasing opportunities for local businesses to supply foodstuffs and other materials to the company's local plants. These tactics enabled the islands' rulers to remain united in the face of the challenges of the liberal nationalists and their more radical supporters and in the end to retain a dominant position within Bahraini society.

Prior to 1955 the state's police force consisted of an assortment of levies drawn mainly from British possessions in South Asia. Its 300 uniformed officers, headquartered in the old fort southwest of the capital,

Police brigade entering Manama fort during the mid-1950s. Source: Charles Belgrave, *Personal Column* (London: Hutchinson, 1960), facing p. 33.

were supplemented by 200 armed watchmen. This force was strengthened in January 1956 with the addition of new personnel from Iraq. Beginning in November, the imperial authorities stepped up their recruiting efforts, this time drawing troops from the protectorates in southern Yemen and the bedouin population of Jordan. The regime also set up a special branch within the police corps specializing in political affairs. This branch was commanded by a British officer seconded to the local administration. Such moves succeeded in creating an efficient, well-equipped police organization on the islands, capable of enforcing the state of emergency declared in mid-November 1956.

Besides the state police, Bahrain's rulers were able to count on the loyalty of the islands' tribal population. Members of clans tied to the Al Khalifah gathered in ar-Rifa' in September 1953 to protect the amir and his family from the rioting in Manama. Two years later a formation of approximately 200 tribal levies was recruited into an autonomous riot squad to deal with internal disorder. This force, drawn largely from clans resident in al-Hasa but allied to the Al Khalifah, was renowned for its ruthlessness in dealing with demonstrators.[27] When the radical wing of the CNU organized the paramilitary scouts in 1956, tribal forces volunteered to engage its cadres in combat and break them up by force.

The regime, not wishing to provoke more widespread opposition to its policies, ordered the tribes to avoid such confrontation.

Sunni tribespeople on the islands remained firmly within the regime's camp during this period not only because of their long-standing connections to the Al Khalifah—several of the larger confederations had accompanied the country's rulers in the invasion of the islands in 1782—but also because the regime allotted their leaders increasingly valuable sections of real estate during the 1920s and 1930s. These properties enabled the tribes to make a comfortable living as rentiers when pearl fishing collapsed and put them in a position to prosper handsomely from the construction boom of the postwar years. As increasing acreage became available through the expansion of irrigation and land reclamation, it was passed on to tribal leaders and other close allies of the ruling family in return for their continued support.

BAPCO contributed to the defeat of the regime's opponents in the mid-1950s by altering its system of securing the provisions and equipment required for its operations. Before 1953, the company purchased virtually all of its supplies directly from overseas distributors, bypassing local import-export firms and circumventing the duties charged on commercial goods coming into the islands. But in the fall of that year the company set up an agency in Manama to handle purchases of food, spare parts and other machinery from Bahraini suppliers. This operation was expanded in 1956 and designated as a "Local Purchasing Department" within the firm.[28] BAPCO expenditures on the domestic market rose sharply after that date. The increase in local purchasing contributed greatly to the regime's success in pacifying the country's smaller-scale tradespeople and splitting moderates within the CNU from more radical social forces.

RECONSTITUTING THE REGIME

In the wake of the nationalist uprising of the mid-1950s, Bahrain's ruling coalition reconstituted itself in such a way as to allow each of the forces within it to maximize its individual interests simultaneously. The country's richer merchants acquiesced in continued autocratic rule, permitting the Al Khalifah to dominate the administrative apparatus created in response to the demands for greater public participation in national policymaking. In return, the ruling family gave the commercial elite free rein over Bahrain's commercial affairs, authorizing a variety of monopolies in the foreign trading sector and requiring outside firms to operate through local agents drawn from the most prominent merchant families. The state administration focused its attention on regulating the labor movement and the network of clubs and religious organizations on the islands, leaving virtually all economic activities in private hands. This revised social compact largely eliminated the conflicts of interest that had generated recurrent friction between the richer merchants and the Al Khalifah from the time the imperial regime was first established.

Members of the ruling family presided over the most important parts of the central bureaucracy in the years after 1956. The administrative council, the labor advisory committee, and the upper and lower courts were all headed by senior shaikhs of the Al Khalifah and included a number of comparatively minor shaikhs as well. By the end of the decade, the key executive posts in the government were held by younger college-educated sons of the ruling family. This trend created resentment among university graduates from nonruling families, whose opportunities for advancement in the civil service were narrowly circumscribed. More technical departments generally employed British expatriates in senior staff positions. During the late 1950s, Britons served as directors of customs, public works, transportation, and agriculture, and a British secretary to the government was given charge of coordinating administrative affairs within the country. Rich merchant representation in the upper echelons of the state was pro forma at best, with appointment to high government office denoting the esteem in which particular individuals or families were held by the amir and his court.

In the economic arena, however, Bahrain's commercial oligarchy carved out for itself a predominant position in the years following the suppression of the nationalist movements. As James Belgrave wrote in 1960, "after a last desperate effort in the autumn of 1956," the country experienced "a considerable increase in commercial and business activities with an attendant improvement in the general standard of living, coinciding with the current period of political apathy."[29] Virtually all of these activities were left unregulated by the government, with committees composed of senior merchants supervising the administration of public works, harbor affairs, and the system of municipal councils. State support for private enterprise was underlined in 1957, when the government set up a free trading zone at Mina Sulman. This move abolished all tariffs and duties on goods coming into the country for reexport, creating a sharp increase in the formation of import-export agencies on the islands. The abolition of all restrictions on the reexport trade was reaffirmed in a port ordinance published in 1964.

As a result of these policies, the foreign trading sector of the Bahraini economy flourished during the decade after 1956. The opportunities for individual enrichment that accompanied this commercial boom effectively defused the explosive political situation of the mid-1950s, as the country's nouveaux riches traders abandoned their efforts to promote economic and administrative reforms and turned their attention to business. In Belgrave's words, "those who were previously in the forefront of political movement, the younger merchants and business men, the educated employees of the government and of commercial organizations and the teachers," became "more concerned with the future and eventual fate of the gulf states and the other Arab countries rather than with day-to-day events in Bahrain itself."[30]

State officials complemented the activities of the Al Khalifah and the commercial establishment by limiting their efforts to expand the scope of the central administration to the areas of labor and club affairs. On 10 October 1957 the government adopted a law regulating industrial compensation; almost exactly a month later the ruler approved a comprehensive labor ordinance. The ordinance mandated a 40-hour work week for the majority of employees on the islands as well as establishing uniform guidelines concerning annual vacations and sick leave. Discharged workers were given a right to reinstatement in the event that their dismissal was found to have been unjustified, and companies were forbidden to discriminate in hiring or retention practices against members of labor organizations.

On the other hand, section 38 of the ordinance explicitly guaranteed a wide range of "management rights," including those of disciplining, suspending and revising pay scales for labor, installing and changing equipment or procedures at the workplace, and "direct[ing] completely the operations of his establishments."[31] In addition, this section stipulated that workers' grievances were to be dealt with on an internal basis, rather than through outside labor organizations. Moreover, according to section 41 of the labor law, firms were permitted to continue their efforts to create joint consultative committees made up of representatives of labor and management to deal with employee relations at local plants. Section 51 held labor leaders responsible for any damage incurred by employers as a result of industrial actions on the part of workers.

In order to enforce the labor ordinance, the regime in early 1957 transferred supervision over the arbitration of labor disputes and the distribution of welfare programs to the director of the labor department. This office had been created in July 1955 but had remained powerless throughout the turbulent nationalist period. In September the ruler appointed his cousin, a former member of the labor advisory committee and senior judge in Bahrain's superior court, as commissioner of labor. In his new capacity, Shaikh 'Ali bin Ahmad was empowered to interpret the labor ordinance, form arbitration committees, and supervise the trades unions. The creation of a centralized labor administration provided the regime with "the tools to cope with . . . labor problems, no matter what the origin,"[32] while leaving private industry free from government restrictions.

State regulation of Bahrain's social and cultural societies crystalized in 1959 with the adoption of an ordinance licensing these organizations. This law required clubs to renounce any involvement in politics, submit the names and addresses of their members to government officials for approval, designate regular meeting times, and limit their recruitment to specific villages or urban districts. Because the ordinance specified no minimum size on the membership of clubs, the number of independent societies on the islands rose dramatically during the late 1950s and early 1960s. The authorities encouraged this proliferation of clubs by refusing to license any organization whose proposed membership crossed community lines. In this way, the regime precluded the formation of a unified network of social-cultural organizations such as the one that had led the Arab nationalist movement of the mid-1950s.

Opponents of the Al Khalifah and its allies thus found themselves facing a considerably stronger and more coherent regime in the aftermath of the liberal nationalist period. The ruling family remained the dominant political force in Bahraini society, exerting its influence not only directly through tribal relations of authority and command over the state's police forces but also indirectly through control of the growing central administration. At the same time, the richer merchants took the lead in directing the country's commercial and financial affairs. Bahrain's private businesspeople took advantage of the regime's laissez-faire orientation to invest a portion of their profits in industrial concerns during the later 1950s as well, leading the Chamber of Commerce to begin registering newly established manufacturing enterprises in 1961. State administrators provided the foundation for private commercial and industrial expansion by keeping the activities of workers and club members under strict supervision. Under these circumstances, programs carried out by any one of these forces reinforced the position of the other two, substantially reducing the potential for conflict both within the dominant coalition and between the regime and its adversaries.

NOTES

1. G. Dalyell, "The Persian Gulf," *Journal of the Royal Central Asian Society* 25(July 1938), p. 357.

2. Ian J. Seccombe, "Labour Migration to the Arabian Gulf: Evolution and Characteristics 1920–1950," *Bulletin of the British Society for Middle East Studies* 10(1983), p. 8.

3. Robin Bidwell, "Bahrain in the Second World War," *Dilmun* 12(1984/85), pp. 34, 36.

4. Ibid., p. 37.

5. For a summary of the strikers' demands, see Mohammed Ghanim al-Rumaihi, *Bahrain: A Study on Social and Political Changes Since the First World War* (Kuwait: University of Kuwait Press, 1975), pp. 119–121.

6. Ibid., p. 105.

7. These stories are drawn from material presented in Michael Field, *The Merchants: The Big Business Families of Saudi Arabia and the Gulf States* (Woodstock, N.Y.: Overlook Press, 1985), and Molly Izzard, *The Gulf: Arabia's Western Approaches* (London: John Murray, 1979).

8. Leigh White, "Allah's Oil: World's Richest Prize," *Saturday Evening Post* 221(27 November 1948), p. 31.

9. James H. D. Belgrave, "Oil and Bahrain," *World Today* 7(February 1951), p. 78.

10. Willard A. Beling, "Recent Developments in Labor Relations in Bahrayn," *Middle East Journal* 13(Spring 1959), p. 158.

11. Ibid., p. 159; Seccombe, "Labour Migration," p. 10.

12. Al-Rumaihi, *Bahrain*, pp. 282–283.

13. Charles Belgrave, *Personal Column* (London: Hutchinson, 1960), p. 144.

14. Fuad I. Khuri, *Tribe and State in Bahrain* (Chicago: University of Chicago Press, 1980), pp. 155–173.

15. Stephen Hemsley Longrigg, *Oil in the Middle East* (London: Oxford University Press, 1961), p. 217.

16. Richard H. Sanger, *The Arabian Peninsula* (Ithaca, N.Y.: Cornell University Press, 1954), p. 147.

17. Rupert Hay, *The Persian Gulf States* (Washington, D.C.: Middle East Institute, 1959), p. 365.

18. Benjamin Shwadran, *The Middle East, Oil and the Great Powers* (New York: Praeger, 1955), p. 378.

19. White, "Allah's Oil," p. 63.

20. Khuri, *Tribe and State*, pp. 199–214.

21. Ibid., p. 202.

22. Al-Rumaihi, *Bahrain*, pp. 289, 290.

23. Khuri, *Tribe and State*, pp. 204–205.

24. Al-Rumaihi, *Bahrain*, p. 296.

25. Khuri, *Tribe and State*, p. 208.

26. Ibid., p. 212.

27. Ibid., p. 122.

28. Al-Rumaihi, *Bahrain*, p. 131.

29. J. Belgrave, "Bahrain, Pearl of the Gulf," *Asian Affairs* (London) 47(April 1960), p. 117.

30. Ibid., p. 124.

31. Beling, "Recent Developments in Labor Relations," pp. 163–165.

32. Ibid., pp. 168–169.

4

Contemporary Politics

Bahrain became independent on 14 August 1971, following Great Britain's decision to pull its armed forces out of the Gulf and a subsequent series of fruitless negotiations over the possibility of creating a federation of smaller Arab Gulf states to replace the British Raj. This event represented a milestone in the country's recent political history, marking the first time in more than one hundred years that Bahrain's rulers held sovereignty over the islands' internal and external affairs. But the coming of independence did little to alter the basic structure of local politics.

In the years since 1971, the country's domestic political arena has continued to represent a paradigmatic case of what Iliya Harik calls an "adaptive patrimonial system." Members of the Al Khalifah constitute the most powerful subset of the Bahraini governing elite, joined by a small but influential group of prominent merchants and professional state administrators. This social coalition relies on tribal authority, control of the central bureaucracy, and—when necessary—armed force to maintain its predominant position within local society. But the regime has also experimented with parliamentary politics and other liberal reforms in an effort to undercut or coopt radical challenges to its continued rule. These experiments were terminated when the regime's opponents began to criticize fundamental aspects of its internal security policies. As a result, popular participation in Bahraini politics in the 1980s has been restricted to closely supervised contests for representation in the workers' councils that have been set up in the country's larger industrial establishments and the largely uncoordinated activities of underground radical and sectarian organizations.

THE AL KHALIFAH

Shaikh 'Isa bin Sulman Al Khalifah (born 4 June 1933) became Bahrain's eleventh amir, or head of the ruling Al Khalifah family, on 16 December 1961 following the death of his father. The succession was

Shaikh 'Isa receiving members of the new Women's Police Corps. Source: State of Bahrain, Ministry of Information, *al-Bahrain: 'ala Tariq at-Taqaddam* (Manama: Government Printing Office, n.d.), p. 157.

uncontested by other members of the royal family not so much because Shaikh 'Isa was the previous ruler's eldest son—primogeniture is far from being an established principle of succession in the Arab Gulf principalities—as because Shaikh Sulman had appointed him heir apparent in 1958. According to the constitution promulgated in December 1973, the office and title of amir are now to be passed automatically from father to eldest son unless the ruler during his lifetime specifies another member of the Al Khalifah to succeed him. This article was one of the few contained in the 1973 constitution that was not subject to amendment. Other articles empowered the ruler to act as head of state, to serve as commander-in-chief of the country's armed forces, and to conclude treaties and other international agreements by decree.

Close relatives of the amir occupy the most important posts in the country's cabinet. In the late 1970s, the ruler's brother, Shaikh Khalifah bin Sulman, held the office of prime minister; his son, Shaikh Hamad bin 'Isa, served as minister of defense; his first cousins, Shaikh Muhammad bin Khalifah and Shaikh Muhammad bin Mubarak, were the ministers of the interior and foreign affairs, respectively; and his second cousins, Shaikhs 'Abd al-'Aziz and 'Isa bin Muhammad, held the posts of minister of education and minister of labor and social affairs.

By the mid-1980s a number of these positions had traded hands, but the distribution of top government offices among different subbranches of the Al Khalifah remained virtually unchanged. Thus Shaikh 'Abd al-'Aziz bin Muhammad was replaced as minister of education by 'Ali Fakhro, the former minister of health and a senior member of one of the country's most influential merchant families; but Shaikh 'Abd al-'Aziz's brother was appointed to the newly created post of secretary-general of the Supreme Council for Youth and Sport, and his nephew Shaikh Khalifah bin Sulman took Shaikh 'Isa's place as minister of labor and social affairs (see Figure 4.1). Members of the Al Khalifah who are not descended from Shaikh 'Isa bin 'Ali, the seventh ruler, occupy subordinate positions in the civil service and staff the middle ranks of the armed forces. A handful of others serve as judges in the state-affiliated, Sunni section of Bahrain's bifurcated judiciary.

Affairs internal to the Al Khalifah as a clan are for the most part handled by a council of elders selected by consensus from among the branches closest to the ruler. This council, presided over by the amir, oversees the distribution of monthly allowances and other economic benefits to royal family members. During the 1970s, its authority has extended to matters of intraclan marriage, divorce, inheritance, debt repayment, and appointment to positions in the civil service. It is also responsible for the Al Khalifah's community property, composed of royal lands whose precise ownership was left undetermined by the cadastral survey of the 1920s.[1] On the whole, this institution has acted to prevent the disintegration of the royal family, by severely limiting the extent of marriage outside the clan on the part of both men and women, by allocating monthly allowances in direct proportion to each family member's relative power and status, and by underwriting the commercial ventures undertaken by the more entrepreneurial individuals within the Al Khalifah.

THE COMMERCIAL ELITE

Prominent members of Bahrain's commercial elite occupy influential posts within the country's most important political institutions, enabling them to maintain a position as vital but junior partners of the senior shaikhs of the Al Khalifah. Three institutions represent particularly

Figure 4.1
Cabinet Ministers Drawn from the Al Khalifah

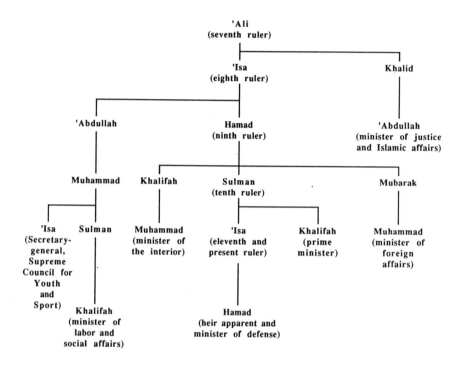

Source: Fuad I. Khuri, *Tribe and State in Bahrain*   (Chicago: University of Chicago
Press, 1980), p. 127, with revisions.

significant bases of power for the richer merchants: the central administration, the municipal councils, and the Chamber of Commerce. Although these agencies are in the end subordinate to the amir and his
closest relatives, each one is permitted considerable latitude in the
planning and implementation of the programs within its purview. As a
result, policy debates among those at the top of these institutions play
a pivotal role in Bahraini political affairs, albeit one that is for the most
part acted out behind the scenes.

Government ministers who are not members of the royal family
are generally drawn from a relatively narrow cross-section of the country's
established rich merchant community, composed of individuals loyal to
the Al Khalifah who have received specialized training in Western

universities. Among the most influential of these officials have been 'Ali Fakru, who has served in a variety of ministerial posts since the late 1960s; Yusif Ahmad ash-Shirawi, the minister of development and industry and acting minister of state for cabinet affairs; and Tariq 'Abd ar-Rahman al-Mu'ayyid, the country's long-standing information minister and a senior adviser to the ruler. Ministerial portfolios have regularly been offered to and accepted by prominent individuals from all segments of the Bahraini commercial elite—Sunni and Shi'a, Najdi and Hawala—in a conscious effort to maintain equal communal representation within the cabinet. A similar balance characterizes the allocation of administrative positions at lower levels of the central bureaucracy as well.

Municipal councils supervise the provision of public services for the six largest urban areas on the islands: Manama, Muharraq, Rifa', al-Hidd, Sitra, and Jidd Hafs. A shaikh of the Al Khalifah serves as the head of each of these councils, but the remaining seats are filled by a combination of methods. In Manama, Muharraq, and al-Hidd, council members are chosen by popular ballot from a slate of nominees representing the more prominent merchant families. In other districts, the central administration appoints local notables to serve on the respective council. Staff personnel are selected according to the peculiar social mix that characterizes each municipality. Consequently, a rough congruence tends to emerge between the actual hierarchy of community power and prestige and the composition of the municipal council, whether the membership of this body is appointed or elected to office.

Finally, the country's Chamber of Commerce represents a crucial but often overlooked force in Bahraini political affairs. By taking part in the deliberations and lobbying activities of this elite organization, the country's most powerful businesspeople can exert a formidable degree of influence upon a wide range of economic and social policies, in effect giving their advice and consent to the state's efforts to deal with matters directly impinging upon their interests. The secretary of the chamber thus serves as a de facto member of the government, although he does not hold ministerial rank. The importance of this institution is reflected in the location of its headquarters in the heart of the capital, adjacent to both Manama Center and Government House.

THE CENTRAL ADMINISTRATION

As recounted in Chapter 3, it was only in the mid-1950s that formal administrative agencies were first established in Bahrain. In April 1955 the ruler appointed a nine-member Labor Ordinance Advisory Committee to formulate a basic labor law for the country. This committee was chaired by one of the ruler's second cousins, Shaikh 'Ali bin

Muhammad, and included another member of the Al Khalifah, a British adviser, three representatives of the local oil industry and three representatives of the country's workers. It was provided with a small staff of its own to deal with legal technicalities and functioned as an advisory body for both the ruler and his British political officer, Sir Charles Belgrave.

In March 1956 a considerably more important administrative body— the Administrative Council—was created, also by amiri decree. This body included 11 members: the chair and 6 others drawn from the Al Khalifah, the British adviser who had served on the Labor Ordinance Advisory Committee, and three prominent merchants, Ahmad 'Ali 'Umran, Salim al-'Urayyid, and Yusif ash-Shirawi. It was charged with discussing and carrying out a limited range of public matters, not including financial and foreign affairs.[2] The bureaucratic structure that grew up around this council during the following 14 years came to include 21 separate departments ranging from a Department of Police to a Department of Minors. These departments were not organized hierarchically. Instead, "all of the 21 departments were placed at the same level; and the head of each reported directly to the ruler."[3] The most important of these agencies was probably the Department of Labor and Social Affairs, as this department was given responsibility for licensing any proposed labor organizations in the country according to the terms of the revised labor ordinance of 1957, as well as all social clubs and societies on the islands according to a 1959 law.

During the mid-1960s, Bahrain's central bureaucracy extended its hold over a wide range of domestic affairs. On 16 November 1963, the ruler initiated the first stage in the construction of a government-planned and -financed community development project given the name 'Isa Town. This stage was completed five years later when Shaikh 'Isa inaugurated the town's first 2,500 houses. In July 1964 the Administrative Council adopted a "Personnel Law" establishing 12 separate categories of state employees, but without setting minimum qualifications or levels of compensation for each category. More significant were the three amiri orders of 22 April 1965 that have collectively come to be known as the Law of Public Security. These decrees empowered the ruler to maintain a virtual state of emergency for an indefinite period of time, to "issue any orders which he deems essential for the public good, safety and security," and to detain anyone "if in the opinion of the Ruler, the detention of [that] person is in the best interest of public security."[4] At the end of July these ordinances were supplemented by a comprehensive press law that both required the licensing of newspapers by the Department of Information and regulated the content of reports published in the press.

Attempts by state officials to regulate the Bahraini economy did not come until later in the decade. In March 1967, the government imposed a tariff on imported tomatoes, cabbages, and cauliflowers in an attempt to protect local farmers from foreign competition. The regime's deep-seated ambivalence toward this sort of state intervention in economic affairs was apparent in its warning to Bahraini growers "that if local production fails to meet market demands or prices rise too high the duty will be removed."[5]

By the early 1970s, Bahrain's state administration was in a position to play an increasing role in the political and economic life of the country. This trend was facilitated by a major overhauling of the organizational structure of the administrative apparatus that was announced by the ruler in January 1970. These measures replaced the existing Administrative Council with a 13-member Council of State.[6] This body differed from its predecessor in two ways. First, it was organized in a more hierarchical fashion, with the heads of the 11 administrative departments and the council's legal adviser reporting to the president of the council, the ruler's brother Shaikh Khalifah, rather than to the amir directly. Second, it contained 10 fewer departments as a result of the merging of existing agencies into more comprehensive ones. Thus, the departments of police and immigration were combined into a new Department of General Security, and the departments of finance, petroleum, housing, customs and ports, and post were integrated to form a new Department of Finance and National Economy.

One of the first actions of the council was to form a National Manpower Council in January 1971 to orchestrate the training and allocation of the country's skilled work force. This committee included the ministers of finance and national economy, labor and social affairs, education, health, defense, and general security. It was provided with a technical staff of experienced civil servants from these departments. The council met periodically over the next two years but never provided its technical staff with a clear mandate for implementing the detailed study of Bahrain's labor situation upon which its deliberations would have to depend. As a result, it had become virtually inoperative by the spring of 1973.

Despite the inactivity of the National Manpower Council, direct state involvement in the Bahraini economy increased substantially during the early 1970s. In March 1972, the islands were chosen by the Organization of Arab Petroleum Exporting Countries (OAPEC) as the site for its joint shipyard project. The Bahraini state took on an 18.84 percent share of the total investment in, operating costs for, and equity of this facility. A member of the Al Khalifah was appointed director of its managing firm, the Arab Shipbuilding and Repair Yards. At almost the same time, three government ministers were given responsibility for resolving the strike against Aluminum Bahrain that had broken out in mid-March. During the course of this commission's meetings with labor and management representatives, the minister of labor and social affairs proposed setting up a network of workers' committees in the country's larger industrial concerns. Elections for membership on these committees were to be supervised by officials from this ministry, and any negotiations between the committees and management were to be carried out under its auspices. Committees of this sort were subsequently set up at both Aluminum Bahrain and the Bahrain Petroleum Company.

Two years later, the government introduced a system of subsidies to moderate the prices of rice, sugar, flour, and meat on local markets. In mid-September 1974, it acquired a 60 percent share in Bahrain Petroleum from its U.S. owners, Standard Oil Company of California and Texaco. State officials announced the following May that they were taking control of the country's internal and international telecommunications system. At the same time, they undertook to acquire a majority holding in Aluminum Bahrain, a goal that was accomplished in early June when the state achieved a 52.4 percent interest in the firm. The next January the government bought out two more of its outside partners to give it a 77.9 percent share of the company's assets.

In the area of labor affairs, a comprehensive labor law was adopted in mid-July 1975. This law prohibited strikes and unionization within the country and mandated instead the arbitration procedures that had been proposed by the minister of labor and social affairs in 1972. A week after this law was promulgated, Shaikh 'Isa ordered the creation of a new Supreme Manpower Council. Among its duties was to be the coordination of efforts by the ministries of health, commerce, education, and development and industry to provide "centralized social projects" for Bahrain's work force.[7] Later in the year, the government adopted a further regulation requiring companies that employed more than 200 workers "to notify the Ministry of Labor and Social Affairs of any vacancies" and receive that ministry's approval before filling any of these openings with non-Bahraini labor.[8]

Substantial increases in the size and scope of the country's central bureaucracy accompanied these measures. In June 1975 the directorate of public health was augmented by the creation of an occupational health and safety section. More important, the ruler greatly enhanced the authority of the Council of State and its component ministeries in conjunction with the government's decision to dissolve the National Assembly. The new cabinet that was formed in the wake of the assembly's dissolution included four new ministries: transport; housing; public works, electricity, and water; and commerce and agriculture. In late November the country's fire departments were similarly reorganized and enlarged; these services were subordinated to the Ministry of the Interior, and their employees were ordered to undergo an extensive retraining program. The year 1975 ended with the promulgation of a new commercial code requiring all trading companies operating in Bahrain to have majority Bahraini ownership and register with the Ministry of Commerce.

Since 1976, Bahrain's administrative apparatus has continued to expand, but at a slower rate. Shaikh 'Isa presided at the opening of the offices of the Gulf International Bank in Manama in December of that year; this institution was set up as a joint venture owned equally by the governments of Bahrain, Qatar, and the United Arab Emirates. In March 1978 the cabinet approved a plan to acquire complete ownership of Bahrain Petroleum's local production and marketing operations. State officials took control of United Building Factories, a local construction and manufacturing company, when the firm encountered difficulties in June 1983. And the Bahrain Monetary Agency introduced new regulations in December 1984 that required money-changers to apply for state licenses in order to do business.

But a certain amount of contraction has also been evident in the scope of the central administration during recent years. In February 1979 the government announced that it was selling 20 percent of Aluminum Bahrain to Saudi Arabia. United Building Factories was leased back to a private consortium in early 1985. Calls for administrative measures to protect local manufacturing firms from outside competition have met with no more than guarded endorsement on the part of state planners. There have been indications that the government might consider selling off its holdings in several of the country's larger industrial enterprises as a way of reducing its growing budget deficits.

Only in the areas of national defense and internal security has the state continued to expand in the 1980s (see Table 4.1). Bahraini officials asked the United States in 1982 to supply the country with advanced military aircraft to serve as the nucleus for a national air force. They were told that this request would be considered only after the country made an initial effort to train its own pilots and build the infrastructure necessary for such a force. By early 1984, the U.S. Army Corps of Engineers was making plans to construct a $100-million military airfield in the uninhabited southern part of Bahrain's main island, and Bahraini pilots were being trained on U.S.-built F-5 aircraft in Saudi Arabia. As a result, the U.S. government in early March 1985 approved the sale of four F-5E tactical fighters, two F-5F two-seat trainers, 60 Sidewinder air-to-air missiles, and support equipment to the Bahraini Ministry of Defense for more than $114 million. An additional four F-5Es and two more F-5Fs were ordered in June. The following November Bahrain

TABLE 4.1
Defense and Internal Security Expenditures, 1974-1983

	Current Expenditures (in $1,000)	Percent of Current Government Expenditures	Total Expenditures (in $1,000)	Percent of Total Government Expenditures
1974	22,538	19.18	22,538	10.91
1976	52,891	22.58	52,891	9.81
1978	90,859	25.00	107,347	14.18
1980	135,788	26.86	158,337	18.93
1981	181,175	29.52	220,019	21.75
1982	223,133	28.20	279,920	22.33
1983	236,430	28.76	287,016	20.33

Source: 'Abd ul-Hadi Khalaf, "Labor Movements in Bahrain," *MERIP Reports* 132 (May 1985), p. 29.

Armored cars of the Bahrain Defense Force on review. Source: State of Bahrain, Ministry of Information, *al-Bahrain: 'ala Tariq at-Taqaddam* (Manama: Government Printing Office, n.d.), p. 152.

agreed to purchase 54 updated M-60 tanks from the U.S. arms manufacturer General Dynamics at a cost of $90 million. At the same time, the government started construction of a chain of modern coast guard stations around the islands, notably on reclaimed land at the midpoint of the Saudi-Bahrain causeway and at Fasht ad-Dibal, midway between Muharraq Island and the northern tip of Qatar. These programs were to be paid for out of a $1-billion fund set up in 1982 by the Gulf Co-operation Council for the purpose of upgrading Bahrain's defenses.

RADICAL CHALLENGES

Bahrain's rulers have faced serious political challenges from three different directions since the mid-1960s. The trades union movement, which had played such a central role in the conflicts of the mid-1950s, continued to pose the greatest threat to the regime throughout the late 1960s and early 1970s. But with the forcible suppression of the wave of strikes that swept the islands in the spring and summer of 1974, Bahrain's labor movement has become markedly less active as a political force. An assortment of revolutionary vanguard parties played a more modest part in local politics during this period. Although membership in these organizations remained relatively small, their manifestoes and communiqués articulated many of the demands of the more radical wing of the labor movement. Finally, after 1978, opposition to Bahrain's rulers became organized along overtly sectarian lines. Militant clerics within the country's Shi'i community mobilized the members of secretive religious associations based in the poorer districts of Manama and its western suburbs to undertake a number of sporadic demonstrations protesting corruption and exploitation in Bahraini society. In the end, the regime has resorted to armed force in suppressing all three sorts of challenges to its predominance, and none of these movements has proved successful in resisting such countermeasures.

Bahrain's second period of widespread labor protest—after the turbulent years of the mid-1950s—was precipitated by a strike against Bahrain Petroleum Company that broke out on 9 March 1965. This action grew out of a series of dismissals of experienced workers at the refinery that resulted from the firm's attempts to automate production. As might be expected, the strikers' demands revolved primarily around the issue of ending layoffs at the company's plants. But the strikers also demanded recognition of the right to unionize, that the state of emergency that had been declared in 1956 be lifted, an end to police harassment, and other matters.[9] Police and military units suppressed this movement during the summer of 1965 and imprisoned or exiled those who had led the striking workers.

Smaller, less well organized protests occurred periodically over the next seven years. Electrical workers walked off their jobs in early 1968 demanding the right to form a trade union, safer working conditions, and salary increases proportional to the rising cost of living on the islands. A series of actions involving workers at Gulf Aviation, Aluminum Bahrain, the local branch of Cable and Wireless, and the departments of health and public works occurred from May to November 1970. The demands voiced by these workers were virtually identical to those expressed by the electrical workers two years earlier.

During March 1972 a more important series of strikes broke out across the country. Workers at Gulf Aviation, the Sulmaniyyah Hospital, the port of Mina Sulman, and Aluminum Bahrain successively walked off their jobs on the 8th, 11th, and 12th of that month. On the 13th and 14th these workers battled police, but on the evening of the 14th they called off their coordinated activities. Their demands were for improved safety procedures on the job, increased wages, and the right to unionize, among other things. Two features of this wave of protests were particularly disconcerting from the regime's perspective. First was the violence to which the strikers resorted. Second was the discipline shown by the protesters in stopping their actions in the face of the government's offer to negotiate with their representatives. By all accounts, this uprising ranks with those of 1954–1956 and March 1965 as the most serious of the country's recurrent labor disputes.

As the debates in the National Assembly became increasingly unproductive, Bahrain's workers began to take direct action to pressure the regime for political and economic reforms. The first half of 1974 saw 24 major strikes on the islands, with the drydock workers holding out longest against government pressure to arbitrate their demands. Aluminum Bahrain employees carried on a series of walkouts and other demonstrations at the company's pressing plant during the summer of that year. Their primary demands appear to have been for higher wages and the reinstatement of dismissed comrades. This strike prompted severe countermeasures on the part of state security forces. Both antiriot police and armed forces personnel were deployed around the Aluminum Bahrain complex in mid-June, and units of the Security and Intelligence Services (SIS) arrested the country's most prominent local labor leaders. At the same time, the regime orchestrated a campaign in the state-regulated press calling for the "elimination of alien ideologies . . . lest the seeds of communism ferment."[10] Moreover, while the National Assembly was recessed for the summer, the ruler issued a "Decree Concerning Matters of State Security," which authorized the minister of the interior to arrest and imprison anyone suspected of "endangering or . . . planning to endanger the security of the state or disturb public order."[11] These measures have been seen as indications that hard-liners within the regime, such as the country's prime minister, used the incident at Aluminum Bahrain to convince more accommodationist forces of the need for more draconian steps to suppress the labor movement.

Although worker militance has greatly diminished within Bahrain since the fall of 1974, it has not disappeared completely. Kuwaiti sources reported a widespread series of industrial actions on the islands in mid-April 1976. Transportation, shipyard, and hospital workers reportedly took part in this wave of strikes, directed against a proposed regulation that would have prohibited them from joining the state-sponsored workers' committees "until they had worked within an organization for five years."[12] Another series of strikes was said to have been under way inside Bahrain the following month. These work stoppages appear to have been undertaken in an effort to force the country's employers to come up with pay increases that would offset the rising cost of living. None of these actions appears to have been as threatening to the regime as the general strikes of 1965 and 1972.

Leftist political organizations have been active in Bahrain since the early 1960s but have generally been less successful than the labor movement in mobilizing broadly based popular opposition to the regime. Between 1968 and 1974, local activists associated with the Arab Nationalist Movement merged with cadres in Oman, Qatar, and the Trucial States to form the Popular Front for the Liberation of Oman and the Arab Gulf (PFLOAG). This organization split in 1974, with the Bahraini section reconstituting itself as the Popular Front in Bahrain (PFB). Support for the PFLOAG/PFB has come primarily from disaffected professionals and intellectuals. The other significant clandestine organizations in the country, the National Liberation Front-Bahrain (NLFB) and the local branch of the Ba'th party, differed from the PFLOAG/PFB less in terms of principles—all of these organizations have claimed to be working toward the creation of a nonexploitative, egalitarian society on the islands—than with regard to more practical matters. The NLFB evidenced pronounced communist, even pro-Soviet, leanings during most of the 1970s and drew its primary support from the more radical trade unionists. The Ba'th, on the other hand, looked to Baghdad for direction and remained a party composed predominantly of the intelligentsia. Such tactical differences prevented the leaders of these movements from cooperating with one another, even when the country's rulers appeared most vulnerable.

Toward the end of 1979, the PFB began negotiating with the NLFB in an attempt to find some basis for joint action.[13] These negotiations lasted more than a year and produced a document entitled "A Common Political Platform," published in January 1981. The platform called for the restoration of parliamentary government and the establishment of independent trade unions. It reportedly has produced some degree of cooperation between these two organizations and the underground labor movement, the Bahrain Workers' Union.

With the suppression of the trade unionists in 1975 and the continuing disarray among leftist organizations, the most serious challenges to the regime have come from Bahrain's heterogeneous Islamist movement. This movement has been usefully characterized by James Bill as "populist," both in terms of its egalitarian principles and in terms of its largely grass-roots mode of organization.[14] In Bahrain, populist Islam has taken two distinct forms: one advocating a relatively moderate, reformist social program and another calling for the overthrow of the existing order, by violence if necessary. The first includes not only the Society for Social Reform (Jam'iyyat al-Islah al-Ijtima'iyyah) and the Supporters of the Call (Ansar ad-Da'wah), whose members are drawn from the islands' Sunni community, but also the Shi'i Party of the Call to Islam (Hizb ad-Da'wah al-Islamiyyah). Most prominent among the second form have been the Islamic Action Organization (Munazzamat al-Amal al-Islami) and the Islamic Front for the Liberation of Bahrain (Jabhat al-Islamiyyah lil-Tahrir al-Bahrain), composed almost exclusively of militant Shi'is.

In August 1979 a crowd of more than 1,000 Bahrainis, predominantly Shi'a, carried out a mass demonstration in the old market section of Manama to voice their support for both the Islamic Republic of Iran and the Palestine national movement. When police detained the organizers of this demonstration, a second march involving some 500 people demanding their release took place in the capital. Faced with this unprecedented display of Shi'i activism, the government deported the leader of the Islamic Front, Hujjat al-Islam Hadi al-Mudarrisi, in October. This move dampened Shi'i political activity only temporarily.

Throughout the spring of 1980, leaders of the Shi'a organized isolated demonstrations to protest the Iraqi regime's execution of Ayatollah Muhammad Baqir as-Sadr, the founder of the Party of the Call. Police arrested a number of the demonstrators, notably the members of the local society that had been headed by al-Mudarrisi, Husain's Fund (as-Sunduq al-Husaini). Their arrests led to scattered ritual mourning processions in the Shi'i villages between Manama and al-Budayya', all of which were intercepted by security forces before they could reach the capital. In early December, political demonstrations broke out in the Shi'i districts around Jidd Hafs. Heavily armed police blockaded side streets and set off cannisters of tear gas to prevent the rioting from spreading to Zarariah, a poorer district of Manama populated largely by unskilled foreign workers.

Almost exactly one year after this incident, on 13 December 1981, Bahrain's Interior Ministry announced that it had uncovered a network of 60 saboteurs operating on the islands. These operatives were reported to be planning a series of attacks on government buildings and high-ranking officials to coincide with National Day celebrations on 16 December. Bahraini police uniforms, sophisticated arms, and large quantities of ammunition were found in three separate caches around ar-Rifa' ash-Sharqi, and the chargé d'affaires at the Iranian embassy in Manama was implicated in the plot. Early in January 1982 security officers named 12 members of the Islamic Front based in Tehran as the leaders of the network. All of these individuals, except for the Iranian chargé who was deported, were indicted at the end of February on charges of subversion and possessing illegal weapons and were put on trial in mid-March. After two months of deliberation, the presiding judge, Shaikh Khalifah bin Muhammad Al Khalifah, handed down sentences of life imprisonment to 3 of the defendants; 15 years each to 59 others; and 7 years apiece to the remaining 10.[15] The efficiency of the state security forces in rounding up these potential Islamic revolutionaries, combined with the evident leniency of the court, severely weakened the indigenous Islamist movement, although a number of smaller cells of militants remain active within the Shi'i community. One such cell, centered in the agricultural district of al-Markh just outside al-Budayya', was quietly broken up by the authorities in early February 1984.

THE PARLIAMENTARY EXPERIMENT

In a public address marking the country's first National Day celebrations in December 1971, Shaikh 'Isa proposed the adoption of a constitutional form of government as a way of enhancing the cohesion of Bahraini society and encouraging a greater level of popular participation in the islands' political affairs. The following June, the amir issued a decree mandating the creation of a Constitutional Assembly charged with debating and ratifying such a document. From the royal family's perspective, constitutional government implied no conception of popular sovereignty or democratic rule. In Emile Nakhleh's apt phrase, the ruler "viewed the Constitution as a gift from him to the people—an expression of royal benevolence."[16] Popular participation was considered at best a form of consultation between those in authority and the ruled, a principle consistent with the tribal-cum-Islamic notion of *shura* (formal consultation between rulers and ruled).

In line with the ruler's mandate, Bahrain's first national elections were held on 1 December 1972. Twenty-two representatives to the Constitutional Assembly were chosen by the country's native-born male citizens 20 years of age and older, grouped into 19 electoral districts centered on the larger urban communities. Several candidates ran for office within each district, with the winner in single-member districts being the candidate who received a plurality of the votes cast. In each of the 3 two-member districts representing Manama and Muharraq, the two candidates with the most votes in each district were declared the winners. In addition to the popularly elected delegates, this assembly included 8 delegates-at-large appointed by the amir and the government's 12 cabinet ministers, making a total of 42 assembly members.

College-educated professionals, middle-income business- and tradespeople, and the owners of the country's newspapers were the strongest supporters of the new electoral system. A month after the law setting up the Constitutional Assembly was promulgated, a group of 15 or so prospective candidates met to decide whether or not to form a unified slate among themselves for the coming campaign. Before such a slate could be put together, one of the more prominent nationalists in the group, 'Abd al-'Aziz Shamlan, pulled out of the caucus and formed a 14-member bloc of his own. At about the same time, another 8 prospective delegates led by Hisham ash-Shihabi formed a third slate, with overtly prolabor leanings.

In late October these three blocs, along with a handful of independent candidates, met to formulate a petition asking the amir to rescind the more draconian provisions of the public security ordinances issued in April 1965. When the cabinet failed to respond to this petition, the members of the Shihabi group pulled out of the election campaign. Purely by chance, the last-minute withdrawal of the Shihabi bloc coincided with a PFLOAG leafleting campaign demanding an end to what was generally called the "state of emergency" in the country. The conjunction of these two events reinforced the suspicions of the more conservative members of the cabinet—reportedly including the prime minister—that instituting an electoral system would only create greater levels of unrest within Bahraini society.

While these groups were jockeying with the ruler and with each other over the question of the regime's internal security practices, professional and middle-income women in the larger cities were mobilizing active protests against the disenfranchisement of female citizens. During the month of September, several women's societies held public fora to decry their exclusion from the electoral process. The most active of these societies—the Bahrain Young Ladies' Association, the Awal Women's Society, and the Rifa' Women's Society—issued calls for public support for women's suffrage that were endorsed by the country's more influential newspapers. Representatives of these organizations asked permission from the minister of labor and social affairs in late September to circulate a petition on this issue; the ministry refused them permission to collect individual signatures on such a petition but allowed it to be signed by corporate groups such as clubs and associations. The resulting document was presented to the amir on 20 November. Shaikh 'Isa reportedly expressed his sympathy for women's rights but did nothing to alter the country's election laws.

Bahrain's commercial elite remained largely noncommital on the issue of establishing a popularly elected parliament and did not participate in the elections, either as candidates or as voters. In a series of interviews given to the Manama weekly *al-Adwa'* in early 1972, several leading merchants expressed guarded support for the notion of a constitution but emphasized that the purpose of such a compact was to enhance cooperation between rulers and ruled. All of these men associated constitutional government with the rule of law and saw a formal constitution as a symbol of Bahrain's national independence. But most of them also were of the opinion that the country was not ready for political parties or a loyal opposition as a component of the policymaking process. Employees of the state administration joined the richer merchants in remaining aloof from the electoral process; according to the electoral statute, government officials were required to resign their posts in order to run for seats in the assembly.

As neither the primary components of the country's ruling social coalition—the Al Khalifah, the richer merchants, and the state administrators—nor some of its most influential challengers—such as the Shihabi bloc and the female citizenry—participated in the Constitutional Assembly elections, the election results indicate two basic trends within sectors of male Bahraini society that usually remain for the most part hidden from view. In the first place, the outcome of these elections tended to reflect the social character of the country's different electoral districts. In Manama, 7 of the 8 successful candidates were from the Shi'i community; the lone exception was a younger member of the Fakri family. In Muharraq, 5 of the 6 winners were Sunnis. Jidd Hafs, al-Budayya', Dumistan, 'Ali, and Sitra all elected Shi'i representatives; 'Isa Town and ar-Rifa' elected Sunni delegates. Nine of the 15 members from Manama, Muharraq and 'Isa Town were professionals; Sitra, ar-Rifa', and Dumistan returned traders; Jidd Hafs and al-Budayya' elected local mullahs; 'Ali sent a prominent labor contractor.

Second, wherever there was a choice between a more liberal candidate and a more conservative one, the conservative usually won. Nakhleh reports that Shi'i candidates often campaigned in local mosques, mullahs running for assembly seats disparaged the devotion of their opponents, and Arab candidates alluded sarcastically to the dialect spoken by their Hawala or Persian rivals.[17] Liberal nationalists with reputations for having struggled against British rule in the 1950s provided the major exceptions to this pattern.

Appointees to the assembly were drawn almost entirely from Bahrain's established commercial elite. Among the at-large delegates, five were influential Sunni merchants: Ahmad 'Ali Kanu, Muhammad Yusuf Jalal, Tariq 'Abd ar-Rahman al-Mu'ayyid, Rashid 'Abd ar-Rahman Qayani, and Ibrahim Hasan Kamal. The remaining three were prominent Shi'i magnates: Ibrahim al-'Urayyid, Muhammad Hasan Khalil Dawani, and Sadiq Muhammad al-Baharna. Some of these families gained additional representation through the ex officio inclusion of the cabinet within the assembly. Dr. 'Ali Fakru, Dr. Husain al-Baharna, and Jawad Salim al-'Urayyid were serving at this time as ministers of health, of state for legal affairs, and of state for cabinet affairs, respectively. On the whole, these appointed delegates voted as a bloc supporting the government's position in the assembly's deliberations, thereby insuring that the resulting constitution would be in line with the wishes of the regime.

Almost exactly one year after beginning its deliberations, the Constitutional Assembly approved a draft constitution consisting of more than 100 articles and passed it on to the amir for enactment. This document envisaged the establishment of a National Assembly consisting of both elected and appointed members. The assembly would serve at the pleasure of the ruler, who was empowered to dissolve it by decree, provided only that he made public the grounds for doing so. If the assembly were dissolved, the constitution mandated new elections within two months; failure to hold new elections invalidated the dissolution and reinstated dismissed members to their seats.

Under the terms set down in this constitution, National Assembly elections took place on 7 December 1973. These elections resembled those of the previous year in several respects: The Shamlan and other personalist blocs having liberal nationalist leanings made up the greatest proportion of candidates; the country's commercial elite abstained from participating; and the PFLOAG boycotted the proceedings. But in other ways they differed from the constitutional assembly elections: Activists of the radical NLFB formed an alliance with several independent leftists, forming the People's Bloc, 8 of whose 12 candidates won assembly seats; a younger member of the Al Khalifah entered himself as a candidate for ar-Rifa' district against the family's wishes, winning a seat in the assembly but acquiring the epithet "the red shaikh" for his impertinence; and Shi'i fundamentalists, supported by the community's religious hierarchy, coalesced into a united front that was successful in beating out the more moderate of their coreligionists.

Three broad coalitions emerged within the assembly shortly after it convened in mid-December. The first of these, the People's Bloc, advocated traditional labor demands for unionization, worker participation in economic policymaking, and higher wages. Its supporters were to be found in the poorer districts of Manama and Muharraq, where workers and students active in the NLFB, the local branch of the Ba'th party, and other radical organizations were concentrated. The Religious Bloc also supported a wide range of labor reforms but insisted that these measures be tied to puritanical restrictions on the licensing of nonreligious youth clubs, the sale of alcoholic beverages, and the interaction between men and women in public places. This bloc's supporters could be found in rural and suburban districts in which the Shi'a made up a majority of the population. Finally, the Independents advocated a variety of programs that were generally in line with the maintenance of an unregulated market economy on the islands and the furtherance of their own vested interests. These representatives formed a heterogeneous group both in terms of social background and in terms of their basis of support. Thus, it is virtually impossible to draw up a composite picture of this particular grouping.

Despite the fact that the National Assembly was authorized only to give advice and consent to laws initiated in the cabinet, and not to propose legislation on its own, its members began to debate two extremely volatile issues during the course of its first year in office. One issue was the formulation of a general labor law that would have allowed trade unions to organize and would have put severe limitations on the importation of foreign workers. The other was the continuation of the internal security measures legitimized by the public security ordinances of 1965. Regarding the first issue, the Independents and the government's representatives in the assembly presented a united front firmly opposed to any measure that might increase the bargaining position of workers within the Bahraini economy. Regarding the second issue, it became evident by mid-1975 that the People's Bloc and the Religious Bloc acting together could not force the government to cancel its security regulations. At the same time, the cabinet and the Religious Bloc could find little ground for mutual cooperation. Consequently, debates within the National Assembly became hopelessly deadlocked and increasingly heated, soon exhausting the patience of the regime.

When, in August 1975, assembly members failed to ratify both the state security decree and the extension of the lease whereby U.S. naval units made use of facilities at Jufair, the prime minister submitted the cabinet's resignation to the amir. The ruler responded by formally dissolving the assembly, while reinstating the cabinet and granting it "full legislative powers." With this move, Bahrain's short-lived experiment in parliamentary government came to an end.

NOTES

1. Fuad I. Khuri, *Tribe and State in Bahrain* (Chicago: University of Chicago Press, 1980), pp. 236–237.

2. Muhammad T. Sadik and William P. Snavely, *Bahrain, Qatar, and the United Arab Emirates* (Lexington, Mass.: D. C. Heath, 1972), pp. 128–129.

3. Ibid., p. 156.

4. Emile A. Nakhleh, *Bahrain* (Lexington, Mass.: D. C. Heath, 1976), pp. 136–137.

5. *Arab Report and Record* (*ARR*), 1–15 March 1967.

6. Sadik and Snavely, *Bahrain*, pp. 129–131.

7. Emile A. Nakhleh, "Labor Markets and Citizenship in Bahrayn and Qatar," *Middle East Journal* 31(Spring 1977), pp. 147–148.

8. *ARR*, 1–15 November 1976.

9. Nakhleh, *Bahrain*, p. 79.

10. 'Abd ul-Hadi Khalaf, "Labor Movements in Bahrain," *MERIP Reports* 132(May 1985), p. 26.

11. Ibid.

12. *ARR*, 16–20 April 1976.

13. Khalaf, "Labor Movements," p. 28.

14. James A. Bill, "Resurgent Islam in the Persian Gulf," *Foreign Affairs* 63(Fall 1984), pp. 108–127.

15. *Middle East Contemporary Survey 1981–1982*, p. 491.

16. Emile A. Nakhleh, "Political Participation and the Constitutional Experiments in the Arab Gulf: Bahrain and Qatar," in Tim Niblock, ed., *Social and Economic Development in the Arab Gulf* (New York: St. Martin's, 1980), pp. 166–167.

17. Nakhleh, *Bahrain*, pp. 154–155.

5

Contemporary Economic Affairs

Specialized studies of the Bahraini economy emphasize the impending exhaustion of the islands' relatively limited petroleum reserves and the regime's persistent efforts to supplement oil operations with other forms of economic activity. As the oldest oil-producing country on the Arabian peninsula, Bahrain's national treasury relied upon monies generated by petroleum production and refining for the greatest part of its income from the early 1930s to the mid-1960s. But as early as the mid-1940s, substantial quantities of crude oil had to be imported from the eastern province of Saudi Arabia to keep the refinery on the east coast of al-Awal operating profitably. By 1968 revenues from the joint Saudi-Bahraini oilfield at Abu Safah made up more than half of the country's total petroleum-based income.

Consequently, during the years since independence, Bahrain's rulers have pursued a number of interrelated strategies designed to promote the diversification of the country's economy. First, the regime has encouraged the creation of an indigenous heavy industrial sector; this program initially focused on industries linked to oil but soon grew to encompass other forms of manufacturing as well. Second, the regime has tried to attract financial and other service institutions to set up regional offices on the islands; as a result of this effort, Bahrain has become the primary center for banking, transportation, and communication in the Gulf. Finally, the state has supported the expansion of modern farming and light manufacturing enterprises, not only as a way of providing necessary inputs for the domestic heavy industrial sector but also to produce agricultural goods and finished items for export to regional markets. These strategies have given the country a diversified domestic economic base that has served as a model for neighboring states.

Although these different strategies have been pursued more or less concurrently over the last three decades, certain strategies have predominated at particular times. Thus, during the late 1960s the government

93

paid special attention to heavy industry and implemented policies that favored this sector at the expense of local agriculture and fishing. The regime's program of inducing financial institutions to open branches in the country crystallized in 1975 and began to fade as the international petroleum market contracted during the early 1980s. As a result, four distinct phases can be discerned in Bahrain's contemporary economic affairs. Breaking the country's recent economic history down into these four periods helps to clarify both the successes and the setbacks the regime has experienced in its efforts to reduce its long-standing dependence on the islands' rapidly vanishing oil resources.

THE MID-1960s: THE PRIMACY OF PETROLEUM

By 1964 Bahrain's petroleum industry was just over 30 years old. During those three decades, the Bahrain Petroleum Company (BAPCO) pumped more than 315 million barrels of crude oil out of the main producing field at Awali, an amount estimated at between one-third and one-half of Bahrain's total proven reserves. Production levels, which had remained stagnant from 1959 to 1963, rose by almost 10 percent in 1964 and by more than 15 percent the following year (see Figure 5.1). Oil revenues provided the government with approximately 75 percent of its annual income, whereas the second greatest source of state revenues—customs duties levied on the country's foreign trade—represented only about 15 percent.[1] The government anticipated that these revenues would increase sharply in the years after 1964 as a result of negotiations between Gulf oil-producing countries and the major international petroleum firms that resulted in royalty payments to host governments being calculated in the same manner as other operating costs—a move that raised each government's share of the profits from the exploitation of oil resources under its jurisdiction to just over 50 percent.

Economic cooperation between Bahrain and Saudi Arabia reached unprecedented levels in the mid-1960s, with petroleum serving as the focus of this collaboration. Beginning in the late 1930s, Saudi crude oil had been shipped to Bahrain for refining and export overseas. By 1962, Saudi Arabia was supplying more than 80 percent of the throughput for the islands' refinery and paying the Bahraini government a toll of almost $4 million per year to transport its oil to the facility. These totals dropped between 1963 and 1967 as BAPCO closed down various sections of the refinery for repair and modernization. But as direct transfers of Saudi crude oil declined, a more important source of Bahraini-Saudi cooperation appeared.

Figure 5.1

Bahraini Petroleum Production, 1955-1985
(in 1,000 barrels)

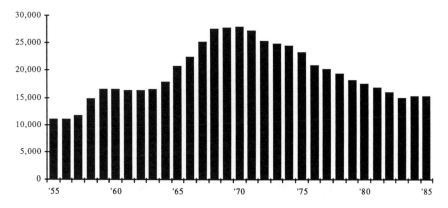

Source: George Lenczowski, *Oil and State in the Middle East* (Ithaca: Cornell University Press, 1960), p. 361; State of Bahrain, *Statistical Abstract* (Manama: Central Statistics Organisation, various years); *Petroleum Economist*, various issues; see also Mohammed Ghanim al-Rumaihi, *Bahrain: A Study on Social and Political Changes Since the First World War* (Kuwait: Kuwait University Press, 1975), p. 99.

In June 1963, the Arabian-American Oil Company (ARAMCO) discovered a major deposit of petroleum at Abu Safah, approximately 25 miles (40 kilometers) to the north of the Saudi port at Dammam. Under the terms of a February 1958 agreement between the rulers of the two states, the Bahraini government ceded this area to Saudi Arabia with the stipulation that any profits derived from the exploitation of oil resources found within it be divided between the two governments. Consequently, when commercial production at the Abu Safah field commenced in December 1965, 50 percent of the profits were allocated to ARAMCO and 25 percent each went to the Saudi and Bahraini treasuries.[2] These revenues provided the basis for a substantial increase in the size of the Bahraini ruler's privy purse beginning in 1966. According to one estimate, the proportion of annual available oil revenues allocated to the ruling family jumped from around 27 percent in 1960 to 36 percent in 1970, with the greatest absolute increase occurring in the period 1966–1970.[3] The petroleum sector thus provided the largest component not only of Bahrain's national economy as a whole but also of the Al Khalifah's own resources during the mid-1960s.

But petroleum was not the only significant economic arena within the country at this time. As early as 1954, a modern ship-repair yard

Fluid catalytic cracking unit at BAPCO refinery circa 1955. Source: Rupert Hay, *The Persian Gulf States* (Washington, D.C.: The Middle East Institute, 1959), p. 75.

capable of handling vessels of 2,000 dead weight tons (2,200 dead weight metric tons) was set up just south of the Manama-Muharraq causeway. This enterprise, Bahrain Ship Repairing and Engineering Company, involved almost 700 local shareholders, led by the Yusuf bin Ahmad Kanu group, whose members owned 51 percent of the company. It was complemented in the mid-1950s by a papermaking factory and a variety of other light manufacturing operations. By 1961, there were 5 soft drink and beverage plants on the islands, 2 tile factories, 6 factories for the manufacture of cement blocks, 3 for plastic manufacturing, and 21 smaller industrial workshops. Between 1961 and 1965, these were joined by 2 more beverage plants, 3 additional tilemaking factories, 9 block factories, and 12 other workshops.[4] Except for the relatively large ship-repairing and plastics enterprises, the great majority of these manufacturing concerns were small in scale and owned by individual proprietors.

Small but dynamic enterprises also made up the commercial sector of the Bahraini economy during the mid-1960s. Local traders received a boost from the government in 1962 with the opening of a free trade area at the port of Mina Sulman. Two years later, state officials issued a port ordinance abolishing all tariffs on goods reexported from Mina Sulman and replacing these duties with a uniform handling charge considerably lower than those in place at other Gulf ports. As a consequence of these administrative measures, the value of reexports from the port rose 15 percent from 1962 to 1966, after suffering a slight drop in the troubled year 1965. According to James Belgrave, director of the *Gulf Mirror* and son of the British adviser of the 1930s and 1940s, there were at this time "some 4,000 commercial establishments, one for every 28 inhabitants" on the islands. It was in fact his opinion that "the importance of trade and things commercial has caused the growth of a middle class of merchants and traders who have helped to make Bahrain the pace setter in the Gulf."[5] Assuming his estimation to be correct, there were more than 50 times as many commercial concerns doing business in the country in the early 1960s as there were manufacturing firms.

Bahrain's trade in this period was quite highly concentrated, both in terms of customers and in terms of suppliers. Muhammad al-Rumaihi reports that the six states of Saudi Arabia, Qatar, Kuwait, Dubai, Abu Dhabi, and Oman accounted for almost 81 percent of Bahraini exports in 1966.[6] Of these customers, Saudi Arabia was by far the largest. The kingdom received almost 52 percent of the value of goods exported from Mina Sulman in 1967, whereas Qatar and Kuwait took in just under 12 percent and 7 percent, respectively. As oil production took off in Abu Dhabi during the early 1960s, Bahraini traders became increasingly active in this market as well, although the nearby entrepôt at Dubai succeeded in capturing the greatest share of this amirate's foreign trade by the middle of the decade. On the other end of this commercial network, the United Kingdom and the United States accounted for almost 40 percent of Bahrain's imports in the mid-1960s, although Japan replaced the United States as the country's second largest trading partner after 1968.

Agriculture and fishing remained important but declining components of the country's economy in the mid-1960s. Large areas previously devoted to date palm cultivation had been converted to vegetable growing at the end of the previous decade, and the still substantial number of native Bahrainis employed as agricultural workers was supplemented by growing numbers of Omani laborers in the years prior to 1965. Citrus fruits, cereals, and fodder crops, particularly alfalfa, constituted the other major crops grown on the islands in these years.

Three features of Bahrain's domestic economy made agriculture increasingly precarious as a source of income as the 1960s went by. First, the growth of the country's urban areas and the resulting demand for land sent real estate values soaring during the middle years of the decade. As Manama spread to the west and south, many of the best plots of agricultural land were sold for commercial and residential development. Second, the inexorable decline in Bahrain's artisanal fishing and pearling industries that accompanied the introduction of large-scale commercial fishing and the importation of cultured pearls into the Gulf substantially reduced the domestic demand for dried dates (which were used as food by the fisherfolk and pearl divers), date palm fiber (which was woven into the ropes used on their boats), and palm branches (which made up the primary building material used in constructing stationary fishtraps). This trend encouraged local farmers to shift from date palm cultivation to vegetable and fruit growing, a move that put significantly greater demands on Bahrain's already scarce supplies of fresh water. Finally, the regime's policy of unrestricted trade encouraged local merchants to import vegetables and fruits from other parts of the Middle East and South Asia, driving down the prices of foodstuffs and making it virtually impossible for domestic producers to compete on local markets. As a result, agriculture became increasingly unprofitable for indigenous farmers, and lands that had been worked productively in the early 1960s began by the middle of the decade to be transformed into nonproductive country estates owned by more prosperous towns-people.

1966–1975: CREATING LARGE-SCALE INDUSTRY

Bahrain's first wave of industrial expansion outside the petroleum-producing sector took place in the two years from 1966 to the end of

1968. During this relatively brief period, officials of the country's central administration joined with members of the commercial elite in setting up a wide range of large-scale, capital-intensive enterprises. Virtually all of these enterprises were designed and built by outside contractors using imported equipment and expatriate labor. Consequently, the establishment of a modern manufacturing sector in Bahrain has not been accompanied by a greater capacity for industrial self-sufficiency. But it has recreated a relatively highly diversified economic structure within the country and provided a basis for continued industrial expansion in the postpetroleum era unmatched among the smaller Gulf states.

This period of industrial development began with the formation of the Bahrain Fishing Company, a consortium that included the Ross Group of Great Britain (with a 40 percent interest) and almost 1,200 local shareholders. The company began operations in the fall of 1966 with a fleet of eight modern shrimping vessels that concentrated their activities in the waters of the north-central Gulf. On 15 March the firm opened a state-of-the-art processing plant at Umm al-Hassam to freeze locally harvested prawns for shipment to markets in Europe, Japan, and the United States. This facility enabled the company to take advantage of record catches during the 1967–1968 season to post a profit of almost BD (Bahraini dinars) 55,000 ($145,000), reversing a loss of almost BD60,000 ($158,000) the previous year. Labor for both the shrimping boats and the processing factory came primarily from the northern principalities of the United Arab Emirates and Oman and tended to be migratory.

In January 1967, the British communications firm Marconi announced plans to construct an earth station for receiving satellite transmissions at Ras Abu Jarjur. This project was part of a £2.1-million ($5.9-million) contract between Marconi and the local branch of Cable and Wireless that joined this local station with similar receiving stations located in Western Europe and Hong Kong. As these plans were being drawn up, Shaikh 'Isa and the government's director of customs and ports, Shaikh Muhammad, met with Saudi officials to discuss the possibility of building a causeway to link their respective countries. The causeway was projected to be around 12 miles (19 kilometers) in length and cost approximately $27 million.

But by far the most ambitious of the industrial projects undertaken in the late 1960s was the £20-million ($48-million) aluminum smelter unveiled in London on 1 October 1968. This plant was to be operated by the newly formed company Aluminum Bahrain (ALBA), a joint venture involving the Bahraini government (27.5 percent), the British Metal Corporation and Aktiebolaget Elektrokoppar of Sweden (25 percent each), the Western Metals Corporation registered in Panama (12.5 percent),

Worker operating automated equipment at ALBA smelter. Source: State of Bahrain, Ministry of Information, *al-Bahrain: 'ala Tariq at-Taqaddam* (Manama: Government Printing Office, n.d.), p. 76.

and the London merchant bank Guiness Mahon (10 percent). The smelter, situated just south of the BAPCO refinery, was designed to utilize natural gas from the oilfield at Awali in transforming alumina pellets imported from Australia into aluminum bars. As a way of reassuring its foreign partners of its commitment to the project, the government exempted ALBA's activities from customs duties and income taxes for its first 20 years of operation and assigned its share of the smelter's output to British Metals for marketing until indigenous ancillary industries could be set up. Bahrain's directors of finance, Mahmud Alawi, and of oil affairs, Yusuf Shirawi, served as founding members of ALBA's board of directors. Work was begun on the project in early January 1969, when it was announced that the facility's original capacity of 57,500 tons (63,250 metric tons) per year would be increased to 90,000 tons (99,000 metric tons) per year through an additional investment of £10 million ($24 million).

In addition to this heavy industrial project, a number of light manufacturing firms were set up on the islands during the late 1960s. The most significant of these were engaged in the production of plastics, ceramic tile, and paper products. To close out this flurry of industrial expansion, the Bahraini government awarded a contract worth almost $1 million to the British firm of Thomas Robinson and Sons for the construction of a modern flour mill capable of producing 100 tons (110 metric tons) of flour per day.

Activity in the country's industrial sector consisted of completing these diverse projects and bringing them on line. Then, in the spring of 1972, a second and markedly shorter period of major industrial expansion occurred on the islands. The first new undertakings of this period were a plant to pulverize locally produced aluminum into powder, most of whose product was exported, and a large-scale paint factory. Much more important was the decision by OAPEC to finance construction of a $60-million shipyard on approximately 100 acres (40 hectares) of reclaimed land off the tip of al-Hidd, opposite the site of the former British naval yard. The drydock complex—named the Arab Shipbuilding and Repair Yard (ASRY)—was the first in the Gulf region capable of handling vessels larger than 400,000 dead weight tons (440,000 dead weight metric tons). It was designed and built by the Anglo-Dutch consortium Costain-Blankevoort using 2,000 workers imported from South Korea. This labor force remained segregated from the local population within an entirely self-contained enclave, provided with its own housing, food, and recreational facilities by the contractors for the duration of the project.[7]

For the next two years, the regime undertook little more than the extension and refitting of existing industrial facilities. In early October 1974, BAPCO announced that it was planning to invest some $120 million to enlarge its production, refining, and loading operations at Awali and Sitra. The country's Ministry of Transport awarded a contract worth almost $5.5 million for enlarging the main air terminal at Muharraq later that same month. In mid-November, work was started on six new berths at the port of Mina Sulman, and extensive dredging was carried out to deepen the port's main channel. More significantly, the Ministry of Finance authorized ALBA in June 1975 to raise $10 million for the construction of an extrusion plant to press section lengths of aluminum out of the ingots produced at its existing factory.

As a concomitant of the regime's efforts to encourage heavy industry, both the construction and the commercial sectors of the Bahraini economy expanded substantially during the early 1970s. The expansion of local

Main drydock and warehouses at ASRY complex. Source: State of Bahrain, Ministry of Information, *al-Bahrain: 'ala Tariq at-Taqaddam* (Manama: Government Printing Office, n.d.), p. 82.

construction is evident in the dramatic increase in that sector's contribution to the gross domestic product (GDP) that took place during the first half of the decade. In 1970, construction represented less than 2 percent of Bahrain's GDP; by 1975, it constituted more than 10 percent (see Table 5.1). At the same time, the proportion of workers engaged in this sector jumped from 17.3 percent in 1971 to 24.9 percent in 1979 (see Table 5.2). Many of these laborers were immigrants, with a large number coming from South Asia and Oman.

Foreign trade expanded at a somewhat less hectic pace between 1970 and 1975. During these five years, the proportion of Bahrain's GDP deriving from this sector of the economy rose from just over 5 percent to just under 9 percent. This increase was apportioned almost equally between imports and exports: Imports grew at a rate of 41.4 percent

TABLE 5.1
Bahrain's Gross Domestic Product by Area of Economic Activity, 1970-1983
(in percent)

	1970	1971	1972	1973	1974	1975	1976	1977	1978	1979	1980	1981	1982	1983
Agriculture	0.9	1.0	1.0	2.5	2.2	2.8	2.2	2.1	2.1	1.4	1.2	1.2	1.2	1.2
Mining	75.8	71.8	66.0	47.9	47.7	38.9	36.6	35.0	32.8	26.6	33.7	29.8	26.0	21.6
Manufacturing	0.9	2.4	4.7	10.7	9.4	10.5	11.4	11.4	9.5	16.4	16.3	16.0	12.2	12.7
Electricity	1.6	1.7	1.7	1.4	1.1	0.8	0.8	0.6	0.7	1.1	0.9	1.1	1.2	1.4
Construction	1.7	1.9	2.2	8.0	8.9	10.3	11.0	13.9	13.2	10.0	7.6	7.8	8.6	10.4
Trade	5.4	5.5	5.6	9.0	7.7	8.7	8.4	8.2	8.7	14.2	12.7	11.4	12.5	12.8
Transportation	0.8	1.3	1.9	5.3	5.5	7.1	6.8	6.1	6.8	10.0	8.7	9.4	10.5	12.0
Finance	4.3	4.8	5.6	2.5	2.9	3.0	6.8	7.6	9.1	9.8	11.0	14.9	18.5	18.0
Real estate	2.9	3.3	3.9	8.5	8.5	9.9	8.2	7.8	8.6	7.0	5.2	6.0	6.6	7.4
Public services	5.6	6.3	7.2	4.2	6.1	8.0	7.6	7.1	8.4	3.3	2.7	2.7	2.5	2.6

Source: Atif Kubursi, *The Economies of the Arabian Gulf: A Statistical Source Book* (London: Croom Helm, 1984), p. 5; United Nations Economic and Social Commission for Western Asia, *Statistical Abstract of the Region of the Economic and Social Commission for Western Asia 1974-1983* (Baghdad: UNESCWA, 1985), p. 22.

TABLE 5.2
Structure of Bahrain's Economically Active Population, 1965-1982
(in percent)

	1965	1971	1979	1981	1982
Agriculture	8.7	6.6	3.4	2.7	2.6
Mining	0.3	0.2	3.1	3.5	0.6
Manufacturing	0.8	13.9	9.0	8.2	11.7
Construction	15.6	17.3	24.9	21.0	20.4
Electricity	19.6	2.8	1.5	2.0	1.6
Commerce	14.5	12.8	12.2	13.6	14.0
Transportation	10.3	12.8	10.8	9.5	10.3
Finance		1.8	3.4	3.6	5.0
Services	17.2	30.4	28.9	34.4	32.1
Not adequately described	9.7	0.2	2.7	1.6	1.6
Unemployed	3.3	1.2			

Source: International Labor Office, *Yearbook of Labor Statistics,* various issues.

from 1970 to 1975, whereas exports showed a rate of increase of 38 percent (see Table 5.3). Most of the goods coming into the country consisted of capital goods such as machinery and building supplies; foodstuffs, which had made up more than 20 percent of the total value of Bahrain's imports in 1970, accounted for less than 7 percent five years later (see Table 5.4). Most of these imports were handled by private firms, creating ample opportunity for the country's merchant community to share in the general economic upturn that accompanied the first wave of industrialization.

Agriculture and fishing fared considerably worse during the early 1970s. By the time of the 1974/75 agricultural census, only about 9,250 acres (3,700 hectares) of the islands' 15,000 acres (6,000 hectares) of arable land remained classified as agricultural holdings, with less than half of this area actively under cultivation. Of these holdings, around 60 percent were leased by their owners on a short-term basis, largely to non-Bahraini tenants. Another 19 percent were composed of very small holdings, each consisting of less than 2.5 acres (1 hectare). Particularly indicative of the precipitous decline of local agriculture were the estimated 475,000 abandoned date palms in the country, along with the finding that about 40 percent of the remaining palm trees were unable to bear fruit.[8]

TABLE 5.3
Average Annual Growth Rates for Exports and Imports, 1950-1983
(in percent increase or decrease)

	Exports	Imports
1950-60	4.2	4.7
1960-70	2.7	1.9
1970-80	30.9	30.9
1970-75	38.0	41.4
1975-83	17.1	15.2
1975-76	20.8	44.2
1976-77	33.1	21.5
1977-78	2.6	0.8
1978-79	31.4	21.3
1979-80	44.6	40.4
1980-81	20.8	18.4
1981-82	-12.8	-12.4
1982-83	-15.6	- 7.5

Source: United Nations Conference on Trade and Development, *Handbook of International Trade and Development Statistics*, Supplement 1985 (New York: United Nations, 1985), pp. 20-21.

TABLE 5.4
Structure of Bahraini Imports, 1970-1982
(as percent of total value of imports)

	1970	1975	1978	1979	1980	1982
Foodstuffs	20.4	6.4	8.1	8.3	6.9	6.2
Agricultural goods	1.2	0.5	0.9	0.5	0.6	0.5
Fuels	1.1	50.8	43.3	51.5	58.3	52.6
Ores	6.3	3.4	2.3	2.1	3.3	3.3
Manufactures	70.6	38.8	45.4	37.4	30.8	37.2
Machinery	29.9	18.8	21.8	17.4	15.0	17.9

Source: United Nations Conference on Trade and Development, *Handbook of International Trade and Development Statistics*, Supplement 1985 (New York: United Nations, 1985), pp. 20-21.

This virtual collapse of date palm cultivation was heralded by a sharp decline in artisanal fishing on the islands as well, as small-scale fisherfolk found themselves increasingly unable to compete with larger commercial concerns. Gulf fishing reached a peak of sorts during the 1968/69 season, when the total commercial shrimp catch was estimated at 16,500 tons (18,150 metric tons) live weight. Subsequent seasons were markedly less productive and by the mid-1970s Bahrain was importing around half a million dollars' worth of fish and fish products for local consumption annually. Most of these imports were brought into the country in frozen form and distributed at subsidized prices by the National Fishing Company.[9]

1975–1982: BANKING ON SERVICES

Economic affairs in Bahrain took a new turn with the government's decision in October 1975 to permit the establishment of offshore banking units (OBUs) within the country. This decision reinforced a substantial rise in foreign banking activity on the islands dating from the spring of that year. On 9 April the country's first non-British European bank opened for business; a month later Canadian Imperial Bank of Commerce opened its first Middle Eastern branch office in Manama. In all, the 14 commercial banks operating in Bahrain recorded a combined profit of BD5.3 million (around $14 million) during 1974.[10] Local officials regarded this upsurge in the country's financial sector as a lucrative complement to the industrial program adopted in the early 1970s and made every effort to sustain it during the second half of the decade.

State involvement in Bahrain's financial sector had begun in 1973, when the government established the Bahrain Monetary Agency (BMA) to supervise currency matters and regulate the operations of local commercial banks. BMA assumed the functions of a central bank for the islands during the first months of 1975 as a result of the government's decisions to entrust it with the revenues from petroleum production and the foreign exchange reserves previously held by the Ministry of Finance. These moves enabled BMA to set the official daily exchange rates for the Bahraini dinar. After taking charge of foreign exchange, the agency gradually extended its control over domestic banking firms, requiring all institutions operating in the country to provide detailed monthly statistics concerning their lending patterns, liquidity, and other matters. Finally, in the fall of 1975 BMA decided to create an offshore area for larger international financial institutions modeled on the one set up by Singapore three years earlier.

Following this model, the Bahraini authorities invited foreign banks to set up OBUs to handle regional transactions and provide on-the-spot information regarding currency flows and lending opportunities to their home bases outside the Gulf. These units were exempted from the exchange controls and cash reserve requirements demanded from onshore institutions, but they were prohibited from dealing directly on the Bahraini market. The program was an instant success: In its first four months, 32 major international banks applied for licenses to establish offshore units; by the end of 1979 more than 50 firms were operating OBUs in the country. The assets of these units rose from approximately $3.5 billion in mid-1976 to almost $16 billion at the end of 1977. By December 1979, the combined assets of OBUs operating in Bahrain reached some $28 billion, a total matching that of Singapore's offshore area. Around 65 percent of these funds represented deposits and loans in U.S. dollars; Saudi riyals constituted another 20 percent of the total. During the late 1970s, approximately 55 percent of the activities of Bahrain's OBUs dealt with the Arab countries, whereas 25 percent and 10 percent involved European interests and Asian concerns, respectively.[11]

Among the primary activities undertaken by Bahrain's OBUs during the late 1970s were the provision of letters of credit to finance imports into the Gulf region and the issuance of bonds guaranteeing the performance of bids and contracts in this part of the world. These activities were of particular importance to Saudi Arabia, but they also served to reestablish Bahrain as a center for the import and reexport of European and Japanese goods to the Arab side of the Gulf. BMA has estimated that each OBU operating in the country brought more than $2 million in annual revenue into the country in the years from 1975 to 1980, making their total contribution to the domestic economy during this period approximately $120 million.[12] Moreover, by late 1979 the OBUs located in Bahrain had lent more than $1 billion to local firms, including sizeable loans to the Bahrain National Oil Company, ALBA, and Gulf Air.

As foreign banks rushed to set up offshore units in Bahrain, construction on the islands boomed. Whereas construction accounted for a little less than 9 percent of the country's GDP in 1974 and employed about 17 percent of the work force in 1971, this sector contributed almost 14 percent of the GDP in 1978 and provided work for almost 25 percent of the economically active population in 1979. In mid-1976 BMA reported that bank loans to the construction sector represented nearly 34 percent of total lending in the domestic economy, a figure indicating that lending to the building industry exceeded lending to commercial enterprises for the first time on record. Most of these projects involved large-scale residential and commercial ventures such as apartment complexes, office blocks, and hotels. Consequently, the construction of smaller buildings on the islands dropped, leading the government to increase the level of public investment in individual housing and other smaller projects in mid-1978.

Heavy industrial investments during the late 1970s remained concentrated in projects integrally related to petroleum and aluminum. At the end of February 1976, for instance, the amir issued a decree setting up a national company for the exploration, refining, storage, transportation, and marketing of locally produced petroleum products. This company, called the Bahrain National Oil Company (BANOCO), was given charge of the state's 60 percent share of BAPCO and further capitalized at BD100 million (about $256 million). Two years later, the government awarded Japan Gas Corporation a contract worth almost $90 million to build a natural gas gathering and treatment plant south of Awali. Most of these projects were financed and subsequently owned by the state, but private companies gradually emerged to complement the larger state-controlled enterprises. By the time the government-owned aluminum extrusion plant began production in April 1977, its first product was purchased by a private Bahraini company to make frames for doors and windows. Another private consortium, headed by the Zayani family, announced plans to set up a $10-million aluminum cable factory that same spring.

In an effort to encourage local businesspeople to invest in small-scale import-substitution manufacturing, Bahrain's Ministry of Trade set aside BD10 million ($26 million) for the creation of the Bahrain Company for Light Industry in the summer of 1979. The company initially consisted of two manufacturing subsidiaries: one for furniture-making and one for the processing of meat sticks. Shares in the firm were offered at BD2 ($5.25) each as a way of insuring that investors would include "the broad base of citizens" and not exclusively "big businessmen or the various companies" already operating on the islands.[13]

As banking and other services expanded on the islands after 1975, increasing demand for foodstuffs provided a stimulus for local agricultural production. Between 1976/77 and 1978/79 total acreage planted in vegetables increased by 12.5 percent. The output of tomatoes, cabbage, and potatoes rose by approximately 70 percent, 11 percent, and 200 percent, respectively. Eggplant, cantaloupe, and cucumbers showed more mixed results, with substantial increases in 1977/78 followed by declines in 1978/79.[14] That much of this growth was achieved through greater mechanization can be demonstrated by the drop in the number of agricultural workers present in Bahrain after 1971 and the jump in imports of agricultural machinery that occurred in the three years beginning in 1975 (see Tables 5.2 and 5.4). State officials encouraged the turn to more capital-intensive farming through the activities of the agricultural research station at al-Budayya' on the western coast. But

Central produce market in Manama. Source: State of Bahrain, Ministry of
Information, *al-Bahrain: 'ala Tariq at-Taqaddam* (Manama: Government Printing
Office, n.d.), p. 10.

even the most traditional agricultural pursuits expanded during this
period as well: Date production, which had languished at around 15,000
tons (16,500 metric tons) per year during the early 1970s, rose to 30,000
tons (33,000 metric tons) in 1976 and then to 38,000 tons (41,800 metric
tons) the following year.

Despite the increase in local production, indigenous agriculture
remained unable to supply most of the necessities for Bahrain's growing
market for consumer goods. The value of imported foodstuffs coming
into the country more than doubled between 1975 and 1977 and continued
to rise until 1981. At about the same time, the value of imported cooking
oils increased sixfold, while that of imported fish products almost tripled.
Conversely, the proportion of machinery imports began to decline during
these years, reaching a low point of 15 percent of the total value of
imported goods in 1980. The continued increase in consumer imports
accompanied a reversal in the pattern of government spending beginning
in 1976, away from capital goods expenditures and toward financing
current accounts (see Table 5.5). In addition to paying for imported
food, these funds were used to purchase the increasing quantity of
imported fuels required by local users; by the late 1970s, fuels from
Saudi Arabia and other suppliers accounted for more than half the total
value of Bahrain's imports.

TABLE 5.5
Distribution of Public Expenditures, 1947/48-1980
(as percent of total state expenditure)

	Current Expenditure	Capital Expenditure	Ruling Family Expenditure
1947/48	48.0	25.6	26.4
1950/51	38.7	32.5	28.8
1955	33.2	37.3	29.5
1960	43.0	30.7	26.3
1965	55.4	22.3	22.3
1970	64.4	6.3	29.3
1973	82.2	17.8	
1974	57.0	43.0	
1975	54.8	45.1	
1976	41.1	58.9	
1977	41.3	58.7	
1978	48.0	52.0	
1979	61.6	38.4	
1980	60.5	39.5	

Source: Ali Khalifa Al-Kuwari, *Oil Revenues in the Gulf Emirates* (Boulder, Colo.: Westview Press, 1978),
p. 80; United Nations Economic and Social Commission for Western Asia, *Statistical Abstract of the Region of the Economic and Social Commission for Western Asia 1974-1983* (Baghdad: UNESCWA, 1985), p. 43; J.S. Birks and C.A. Sinclair, *Arab Manpower* (New York: St. Martin's, 1980), p. 165.

1983–PRESENT: RETURNING TO INDUSTRY

By mid-1982 the rapid expansion of the financial sector of Bahrain's economy that had characterized the late 1970s began to level off. Total assets of the OBUs operating in the country reached $50.7 billion in the last months of 1981 but increased only to about $62.7 billion in December 1983, despite the addition of 10 new units during this period. As the profitability of regional banking slumped and the cost of maintaining offices in Manama continued to rise, several smaller OBUs cut back on both the size of their local staffs and the range of services they provided to customers. As a result, state officials began once again to focus their attention on Bahraini heavy industry and agriculture as potential bases for sustained economic growth.

Three large-scale heavy industrial projects lay at the heart of the regime's economic program during the early 1980s. The first of these is the Arab Iron and Steel Company (AISCO) plant in the Sitra Island industrial complex. This plant, which began operations in December 1984, is capable of producing up to 4 million tons (4.4 million metric tons) of iron ore pellets per year for use in the Saudi steelworks at Jubail. Its parent company is a joint venture of the Amman-based Arab Mining Company and a number of Gulf industrial and financial concerns. The second large project is the aluminum rolling mill at Sitra, owned by the Gulf Aluminum Rolling Mill Company (GARMCO), a consortium composed of agencies of six Arab Gulf governments. This mill has the capacity to produce 40,000 tons (44,000 metric tons) of rolled aluminum sheet and coil. In early 1986 GARMCO was contemplating the addition of a foilmaking facility to this plant to meet the rising demand for aluminum foil and other packaging materials throughout the Gulf. The last of these large-scale projects is the $450-million Gulf Petrochemical Industries Company (GPIC), capable of producing 1,000 tons (1,100 metric tons) per day of both methanol and ammonia. In January 1985 the Bahraini government's partners in this venture, Petrochemical Industries Company of Kuwait and Saudi Basic Industries Company, agreed to handle the distribution of GPIC's products on both regional and European markets.

At the same time these new heavy industrial facilities were being constructed, aluminum production at ALBA began to rise as the industry started pulling out of the slump it had experienced in 1981/82. Record levels of both hot metal output and finished metal production were achieved at ALBA's smelter for 1983 and 1984, with the latter rising to 4 percent over the facility's rated capacity during the second of these years. Also in 1984 income at the associated extrusion plant rose by 18 percent, although a decline in construction on the islands and competition from foreign suppliers of aluminum products created a mild recession in the industry by the end of 1985.

Other components of Bahrain's heavy industrial sector found themselves facing considerable difficulties by the early 1980s. The pronounced decline in Gulf shipping that resulted from lower petroleum exports and the continuing war between Iran and Iraq cut revenues at ASRY to an all-time low in 1983, leading the firm to streamline its operations and begin moving into the areas of steel fabrication and metal construction. By diversifying in this fashion, the company was able to achieve a 24 percent increase in revenues during 1984. BAPCO, BANAGAS (Bahrain National Gas Company), and GPIC all incurred serious losses in this same period as a result of dropping oil prices on world markets. BAPCO's refinery, which was under contract with Saudi Arabia to purchase 70 percent of its feedstock at officially posted prices, found the cost of this crude oil rising relative to that of oil purchased on the spot market even as its products were selling for less on both regional and outside markets. BANAGAS' net income fell by more than 60 percent from 1984 to 1985 as a result of higher charges for feed gas and lower prices for the naphtha produced at the plant. Falling prices also forced GPIC to pare down its operating costs and raise output by 20 percent in 1985/86. But by mid-1986 this strategy had begun to backfire: Higher methanol exports to Western Europe led the Common Market to impose a 13 percent tariff on further imports from Bahrain that June.

In an effort to counteract the adverse effects of plunging petroleum prices on the Bahraini economy, BANOCO initiated a $60-million project to drill 80 new wells at the Awali field beginning in 1986. This move followed the completion of a $4-million modernization project that entailed the overhauling of 130 of the 380 wells operating at the field and the injection of natural gas into the field to raise pumping pressure. In addition, the company continued to expand natural gas production from the adjacent Khuff reservoir, where total reserves were estimated at 9 trillion cubic feet (255 billion cubic meters). Gas pulled from this reservoir was to be earmarked for domestic uses—particularly by ALBA and the directorate for electricity—rather than for export.

Besides oil production, state officials targeted agriculture and fishing as arenas for greater public investment in the mid-1980s. Government agricultural agents put highest priority on increasing local production of vegetables, fruits, and poultry; other goals included the improvement of the country's irrigation and drainage systems. As part of a six-year development program launched in 1982, the state offered farmers subsidies amounting to 40–50 percent on seed, fertilizers, and agricultural machinery and made low-interest loans available for the construction of farm buildings and housing for agricultural labor. By 1985, these incentives had helped raise vegetable and fruit production to the point of satisfying 28 percent and 12 percent of domestic demand, respectively. That same year, the government set up a national dairy company to produce milk for domestic consumption, accepted a comprehensive plan drawn up by the United Nations Development Program to increase the number of fish hatcheries around the islands and stepped up the level of state funding for the installation of sophisticated drip irrigation equipment on local farms.

Publicly supported housing and land-reclamation projects represented a second major area of emphasis in the government's development program. On 15 December 1984, Shaikh 'Isa presided over the opening of the initial 800-house section of Hamad Town. This project was designed to provide housing for 60,000 people, making it almost twice as large as its prototype, 'Isa Town. An even more ambitious project, involving the reclamation of some 50,000 acres (20,000 hectares) of land to the south of Mina Sulman, was undertaken at the beginning of 1985.

State planners envisaged the creation of a third new town capable of housing 70,000 people on this land, designated Fasht al-Adham, along with a coast guard station and a new causeway linking the town to Manama.

Finally, 1986 saw the completion of the 19-mile (30-kilometer) causeway joining the eastern province of Saudi Arabia to the main island of Bahrain. This link to the mainland was expected to create an upsurge in the real estate and tourism sectors of the country's economy. But it was also anticipated that imported goods entering the islands from the much larger Saudi market, particularly processed foods and electronic items, would reduce profits for local distributors and make Bahraini markets considerably more competitive. The existence of quasi-monopoly licenses for many trademarked products was expected to ameliorate the costs of closer contact with Saudi Arabia to some extent.

On the whole, the completion of the Saudi-Bahraini causeway signaled the growing interdependence of the economic affairs of these two Gulf countries by the mid-1980s. Saudi funds made up the largest share of monies funneled through Bahrain's OBUs; Saudi interests constituted major partners in Bahrain's leading heavy industrial concerns; Saudi crude oil represented almost three-quarters of the throughput at the BAPCO refinery. In mid-June 1986, Bahrain Light Industries Company received its first order for office furniture and other fittings—from a Saudi buyer. The following month, Bahrain Flour Mills Company took delivery of an initial consignment of hard Saudi wheat, which it planned to mix with softer wheat imported from Australia to manufacture lower-cost flour for domestic consumption. In short, the Saudi kingdom has begun to play an increasingly crucial role in the Bahraini economy, and the Al Khalifah and its supporters may find it harder to counteract Saudi economic predominance than it was to stimulate diversification into industry and finance as a way of overcoming Bahrain's dependence on petroleum.

CONCLUSION

Despite the impending exhaustion of the country's petroleum reserves, Bahrain's economic prospects appear brighter than those of many of its more oil-rich neighbors. Even in the recession year of 1985 the Bahrain Monetary Agency reported a small overall surplus in the country's balance of payments, despite a drop of almost 10 percent in the value of petroleum-related exports. Activities related to the state-supported aluminum industry provide the islands with a viable alternative to oil, an alternative that promises to become more profitable with the expansion and modernization of the main ALBA smelter due to be carried out in

1988/89. Competition from new plants elsewhere in the region, such as the smelter under construction at Umm al-Qaiwain in the United Arab Emirates, is likely to remain manageable in the near future, given the high start-up costs involved in this kind of capital-intensive enterprise. Meanwhile, local demand for aluminum continues to grow, as the extrusion and rolling mills designed to make use of the materials produced at the smelter reach their planned capacities. Officials at the Ministry of Development and Industry predict that domestic sales will account for 40 percent of ALBA's total output in 1988; domestic sales already accounted for 25 percent of the company's output in mid-1986.

Economic forecasts for the islands remain impaired by the uncertainties associated with trends in the international petroleum market and the aftereffects of the war between Iran and Iraq. Depressed prices have had an adverse effect not only on domestic oil production and refining, but also on such peripheral enterprises as the Gulf Petrochemical Industries Company. Instability caused by the war has not only disrupted regional trade and finance but has also interfered with attempts by local industrial firms to develop regional markets for their products. Cases in point are the iron-pelleting plant belonging to the Arab Iron and Steel Company, which has been unable to follow up on plans to market its pellets in Iran and Iraq, and the Arab Shipbuilding and Repair Yard, whose operations have had to be drastically restructured as a result of the high insurance premiums charged on commercial shipping in the Gulf. These trends cast a gloom over private business and industry on the islands during 1986/87 that government officials made dramatic efforts to dispel. But paradoxically enough, these trends have also enhanced the capacity of local enterprises to adapt to changing circumstances, thereby improving the regime's chances of surmounting future economic crises.

NOTES

1. Ali Khalifa Al-Kuwari, *Oil Revenues in the Gulf Emirates* (Boulder, Colo.: Westview Press, 1978), pp. 90 and 76.

2. Husain M. Al-Baharna, *The Legal Status of the Arabian Gulf States* (Manchester: Manchester University Press, 1968), p. 300.

3. Al-Kuwari, *Oil Revenues*, pp. 84–85.

4. Mohammed Ghanim al-Rumaihi, *Bahrain: A Study on Social and Political Changes since the First World War* (Kuwait: University of Kuwait Press, 1975), pp. 94–95.

5. J. Belgrave, "The Changing Social Scene in Bahrain," *Middle East Forum* 38(Summer 1962), p. 62.

6. Al-Rumaihi, *Bahrain*, p. 92.

7. J. S. Birks and C. A. Sinclair, *Arab Manpower* (New York: St. Martin's, 1980), p. 172.

8. H. Bowen-Jones, "Agriculture in Bahrain, Kuwait, Qatar and the UAE," in May Ziwar-Daftari, ed., *Issues in Development: The Arab Gulf States* (London: MD Research and Services, 1980).

9. William J. Donaldson, "Fisheries of the Arabian Peninsula," in John I. Clarke and Howard Bowen-Jones, eds., *Change and Development in the Middle East* (London: Methuen, 1981).

10. *Arab Report and Record (ARR)*, 1–15 April and 1–15 May 1975.

11. Alan E. Moore, "The Development of Banking in Bahrain," in Ziwar-Daftari, *Issues in Development*, p. 149.

12. Rodney Wilson, *Banking and Finance in the Arab Middle East* (New York: St. Martin's, 1983), p. 115.

13. *Al-Adwa'* (Manama), 4 August 1979, p. 1.

14. State of Bahrain, *Statistical Abstract 1978* (Manama: Directorate of Statistics, September 1979), p. 214, and *Statistical Abstract 1979* (Manama: Directorate of Statistics, October 1980), p. 212.

6

Foreign Relations

In the years since independence, Bahrain's rulers have executed a complex balancing act in pursuit of security and autonomy for the new state. In the first place, the regime has been engaged in a continuing effort to define the character of its strategic relations with the dominant extraregional power in the Gulf. Prior to August 1971, this bargaining involved the traditional protector of the smaller Gulf amirates, Great Britain; after that date it has primarily involved the United States. Second, Manama has had to parry periodic challenges from Iran. Both the Pahlavi regime in Tehran and its successor, the Islamic Republic, have advanced claims to sovereignty over the Bahrain archipelago on the basis of patterns of territorial control that long antedated the British Raj. Bahrain's resistance to these claims has played a major role in shaping the country's regional diplomacy throughout the postindependence period.

Third, Bahrain has devoted considerable attention to the matter of working out mutually beneficial relations with the other Arab Gulf states. Although the country shares a wide range of interests with Saudi Arabia, Kuwait, and the other Gulf amirates, Bahrain has made a practice of playing these states off against one another in an attempt to prevent any of its neighbors from achieving a hegemonic position in regional affairs. Finally, Bahrain's rulers have had to cope with the effects of the war between Iraq and Iran. These effects have facilitated intraregional diplomacy by mitigating tensions among the Arab Gulf states but have also forced Manama into an increasingly subordinate position relative to Saudi Arabia and the other members of the Gulf Cooperation Council. Bahrain's capacity to reassert its autonomy in the wake of the Iran-Iraq war will be largely determined by the strength and resilience of the bonds that have grown up between the country and its partners in this association in the years since 1980. This capacity has paradoxically been augmented by the persistence of boundary and other disputes that pose a latent threat to harmonious interaction between Manama and neighboring capitals.

STRATEGIC RELATIONS WITH
EXTRAREGIONAL POWERS

Over the last 40 years or so, Bahrain has carved out for itself a unique position as the primary, albeit silent, regional partner of the major outside power active in the Gulf. This pattern took shape during the mid-1940s, when Shaikh Sulman encouraged the imperial authorities in Bombay to transfer the headquarters of the British Resident to Manama from Bushire on the Persian coast. The move was implemented in 1946, and the Residency's offices remained on the islands when responsibility for Gulf affairs shifted to London following India's independence in April 1947. Throughout the postwar period, facilities in Bahrain played a crucial role in British diplomatic and military activities east of Suez. The airfield at Muharraq and the naval base at Jufair served as key staging points for Royal Air Force and Navy units dispatched to Kuwait in the summer of 1961, and the British garrison on the islands was further expanded in the wake of Britain's withdrawal from Aden six years later.[1] Beginning in September 1967, command of all British military units stationed in the region rested with the Commander British Forces Gulf based in Bahrain.

Britain's decision to pull its armed forces out of the Gulf in the spring of 1971 strained but did not sever the strategic connection between London and Manama. The withdrawal plan announced by the Conservative foreign secretary, Sir Alec Douglas-Home, that March envisaged the replacement of the existing bilateral defense treaties between Great Britain and the respective amirates of the lower Gulf with a general treaty of friendship linking Britain with a proposed federation of Arab amirates. The new arrangement would have allowed British officers to continue advising local military establishments, Britain to remain the primary supplier of military equipment to the region, and British forces to retain staging and overflight privileges at bases all along the southern coast of the Gulf. In Douglas-Home's words, such an arrangement could "form a sound basis for a continuing and effective British contribution to the stability of the area."[2] U.S. officials, in the meantime, announced that they had no plans to replace British troops in the Gulf with units of the U.S. armed forces.

As the Bahraini government debated whether or not to join the proposed federation of amirates, Britain completed the evacuation of its military forces on the islands. On 18 July 1971 the last two companies of British soldiers left Jufair for the Royal Air Force base at Sharjah on the Arabian coast, and the newly organized Bahrain Defense Force assumed responsibility for defending the archipelago. A month later, Shaikh 'Isa declared Bahrain an independent state with the right to formulate and conduct its own foreign relations. The amir and the British Political Agent–cum–ambassador, Sir Geoffrey Arthur, signed a treaty of mutual friendship the following day that formally ended British responsibility for Bahrain's defense but that reportedly provided for joint "consultation in time of need."[3] Other Arab states generally welcomed the treaty, although it was criticized by the Soviet Union and the People's Democratic Republic of Yemen on the grounds that it masked the "neocolonial" character of Bahrain's relationship with Great Britain.

At the same time British forces were evacuating the islands, Manama began negotiating with Washington over the continued use of docking facilities at Jufair by U.S. naval units. A flotilla consisting of a converted seaplane tender and two destroyers, designated the U.S. Middle East Force, had been stationed at the port since 1949, largely as a symbol of U.S. interest in Gulf affairs. Bahraini and U.S. officials agreed in December 1971 that this force could remain based at Jufair even after the Royal Navy pulled out and that its continued presence at the port implied no military or diplomatic commitment on Washington's part to defend the islands.

Despite efforts by the U.S. State Department to keep these negotiations quiet, reports of the executive agreement between Manama and Washington appeared in the U.S. press in early January 1972. Members of the Senate Foreign Relations Committee, angered that they had not been informed about the new agreement, then resolved that the U.S. government negotiate a formal treaty with Bahrain governing the use of the base. By early April, the Senate had adopted a further resolution cutting off all military assistance to Bahrain until the basing agreement was submitted for congressional approval. When the Nixon administration refused to comply, the Senate voted by a narrow margin to refuse to authorize funds for renting or operating any facilities at Jufair. This move was overturned in the final military assistance authorization bill adopted in late June, when the administration finally convinced the Senate that putting the arrangement in treaty form would create serious difficulties for the Bahraini government in its dealings with other Arab states.

In an attempt to reassure Manama of its commitment to maintain a viable military presence on the islands, the U.S. government dispatched Secretary of State William Rogers to Bahrain at the beginning of July 1972. Before arriving in the area, Secretary Rogers attended the annual meeting of foreign ministers of the Central Treaty Organization (CENTO) in London, informing those present that the United States planned to replace the outdated warships stationed in the Gulf with more modern vessels. The secretary announced at the end of his talks with Bahraini officials that the U.S. Middle East Force would continue to operate out of Jufair and declared that these operations posed no threat to any country, including the Soviet Union, whose navy had begun calling at the Iraqi port of Umm Qasr the previous spring. No further developments in relations between Manama and Washington occurred over the subsequent fifteen months, although the U.S. presence in the Gulf was briefly reinforced in September 1972 when two warships of the Pakistani navy attached to CENTO arrived at Jufair on a courtesy call.

U.S. support for Israel in the October War of 1973 led the Bahraini government to announce that it intended to cancel the agreement permitting the U.S. Middle East Force to dock at Jufair. In early November, as part of the OAPEC boycott of the United States, the Bahraini government cut off supplies of refined petroleum to the U.S. Navy from the BAPCO refinery at Sitra. Relations between the local authorities and the U.S. garrison remained strained throughout the following year. But in early October 1974, sources at the Pentagon reported that Bahrain had reversed its position and decided to allow the flotilla to remain based on the islands.

During November 1974, U.S. naval forces increased their activities in and around Bahrain. The aircraft carrier *Constellation* and two escort ships entered the Gulf the third week of that month on a "familiarization deployment" as part of CENTO exercises in the Indian Ocean; in mid-January 1975 British sources reported that the United States had requested permission to use the undeveloped airfield on Masirah Island southeast of Oman on an occasional basis.[4] These operations caused considerable concern in other Arab capitals: The National Assembly of the newly formed Federation of Arab Republics—consisting of Egypt, Syria and Libya—urged Bahrain to suspend docking privileges for the U.S. Middle East Force on the grounds that U.S. maneuvers posed an "open threat to the Arab oil states."[5] Shaikh Muhammad bin Mubarak, the Bahraini foreign minister, responded by saying that the U.S. Navy's right to use the port depended upon "the American stand concerning peace and stability in the Middle East."[6] Under the circumstances, the United States agreed to a 600 percent increase in the annual rent for its facilities at Jufair. Reports that the United States would evacuate the base nevertheless persisted over the next two years.

At the end of June 1977, the original executive agreement between Bahrain and the United States concerning the use of Jufair expired. It was replaced by a new arrangement whereby the port would no longer be considered the home base for the U.S. Middle East Force, but its warships would be permitted to call at Jufair for supplies upon request. Local observers remarked that this arrangement allowed the U.S. flotilla to reduce its "already low profile" while maintaining a regular presence on the islands.[7] From Manama's perspective, the new arrangement reflected "the constructive approach to the Middle East by the US administration," a continuing need to provide "stability" in regional affairs, and Bahrain's desire to obtain greater access to U.S. technical expertise. On 1 July the commander of the force officially handed over control of the U.S. installation to the Bahraini government.

Relations between the United States and Bahrain have remained for the most part low-key and stable under the terms of the new agreement. The former flagship of the U.S. Middle East Force makes regular use of facilities at Jufair, as do support vessels attached to the U.S. Navy's Indian Ocean task force; U.S. personnel remain stationed at the port to supervise supply operations and provide instructors for a small naval training school. Events surrounding the revolution in Iran put Bahraini-U.S. relations under some degree of stress but left them substantially undamaged: In response to statements by Secretary of Defense Harold Brown in July 1979 indicating that the United States planned to augment its presence in the Gulf and might make use of these units if vital U.S. interests were threatened, Bahrain's prime minister reiterated his government's view that the security of this part of the world was the responsibility of local forces themselves; in the wake of the failed attempt to rescue American personnel from the captured embassy in Tehran in mid-April 1980, demonstrators took to the streets in Manama protesting the alleged use of airfields on the islands by U.S. military aircraft involved in the operation.

U.S. naval forces in and around the Gulf were substantially reinforced as the war between Iran and Iraq escalated during the early spring of 1984 and Iraqi aircraft began attacking oil tankers navigating between Kharq Island and the Strait of Hormuz. By mid-May of that year, the Reagan administration had increased the number of destroyers attached to the U.S. Middle East Force to five and was pushing Bahrain, Kuwait, and Saudi Arabia to designate air bases for use by U.S. naval aircraft tracking unarmed merchant shipping in the area. U.S. commanders deployed three of these destroyers to the upper Gulf in early February 1987 in response to Iranian advances toward the Iraqi city of Basra and growing Soviet involvement in regional affairs. The deployment was intended both to reassure the smaller Arab Gulf states of continued U.S. support and to provide Washington with a viable military option in case Iranian forces moved south into Kuwait or Saudi Arabia.

By the spring of 1987, Bahrain had become the unofficial center of the expanding U.S. presence in the Gulf. Warships of the U.S. Middle East Force were earmarked to play a key role in escorting convoys of reflagged Kuwaiti tankers through the area under the terms of an agreement announced in early April. Six weeks later an American frigate was towed to the islands' massive drydock for preliminary repairs after being severely damaged by an Iraqi air-to-sea missile. Following the start of convoy escort operations in mid-July, the U.S. facility at Jufair was quietly upgraded, and supply flights of U.S. military transport aircraft began arriving on a regular basis at the airport at Muharraq bringing food, mail, and other necessities to the sailors stationed in the Gulf.

As direct U.S. involvement in the region became more pronounced, Washington began encouraging Bahrain to enlarge and modernize its own armed forces. U.S. Army engineers took primary responsibility for finding contractors to build the new military air base south of Awali. In March 1985 the U.S. Department of Defense brokered the purchase of 6 Northrop F-5 fighters, along with Sidewinder antiaircraft missiles and the necessary support equipment, for the Bahraini air force; 6 additional F-5s were ordered in mid-June. These 12 fighters constituted the first fixed-wing aircraft in the arsenal of the Bahrain Defense Force. Pentagon officials announced at the end of the year that Bahrain had ordered 54 upgraded M-60 main battle tanks worth almost $90 million. In early 1987 the Reagan administration informed the U.S. Congress that it intended to supply the country with 12 advanced F-16 fighter aircraft, a weapons system previously supplied only to Israel and Egypt. That spring, Washington made public its plans to sell artillery shells made of spent uranium to the Bahrain Defense Force for use against heavily armored tanks. Each of these sales represented a significant escalation of U.S. efforts to equip, support, and train the regime's armed forces.

Bahrain's strategic relations with the United States have therefore been consistently close in the years since independence. Manama has generally welcomed an active U.S. military presence in the country, despite the criticism this position has generated throughout most of the Arab world. Only when U.S. operations in the Middle East have taken a course diametrically opposed either to the interests of Arab nationalism or to the principle of nonintervention in local affairs has the Bahraini government threatened to terminate the agreement allowing U.S. naval forces access to the port at Jufair. The clarity of purpose with which Manama has dealt with Washington over the last decade and a half has left Bahrain in a strong bargaining position relative to that of the United States and has thus contributed to U.S. willingness to let the Bahraini government set the rules by which U.S. military units operate on the islands.

While cementing its ties to the United States, Manama has consistently rebuffed diplomatic overtures from the Soviet Union in the years since independence. Throughout the fall and winter of 1971–1972, Soviet officials made repeated requests to open an embassy in the country, and each request was studiously ignored by the local authorities.

Moscow's verbal denunciations of the Bahraini regime became increasingly strident following the dissolution of the National Assembly in August of 1975, and Soviet journalists began devoting greater attention to the program and activities of the National Liberation Front–Bahrain after that date. Consequently, the Al Khalifah and their domestic partners have shown little interest in establishing normal relations with the USSR or any other communist state, despite the fact that both parties have adopted identical positions condemning the Camp David accords between Israel and Egypt and the Israeli invasion of Lebanon in the summer of 1982.

CHALLENGES FROM IRAN

Iran's relations with Bahrain have changed dramatically over the course of the last two decades. Throughout most of the twentieth century, successive governments in Tehran have represented the most serious threat to the autonomy of the amirate, claiming sovereignty over the islands on the basis of purported historical connections between the islands' rulers and their nominal overlords on the Persian mainland. These claims were revived in the aftermath of the 1978–1979 revolution, when a respected Iranian cleric called for the incorporation of the islands into the Islamic Republic. Relations between Iran and Bahrain reached a nadir at the end of 1981, when Iranian-supported dissidents attempted to spark a popular uprising against the Al Khalifah. After the arrest of these agents provocateurs, a gradual trend toward accommodation began to characterize dealings between Tehran and Manama. This thaw represented in part a desire shared by all of the Arab Gulf states to reduce the potential for direct confrontation between themselves and the Islamic Republic. But it also illustrated a long-standing Bahraini strategy of manipulating relations with the amirate's more powerful neighbors in an effort to gain the greatest possible maneuverability in regional affairs.

As early as 1927, the Iranian authorities lodged a formal protest against the British government's policy of treating Bahrain as an independent state having special ties to Great Britain. In a series of notes dispatched first to London and then to the headquarters of the League of Nations in Geneva, Iran asserted that the islands had been subject to successive rulers in Tehran throughout the period prior to 1820 and had been forcibly occupied by the British not only in contravention of the wishes of the local population but also over the objections of the Iranian government of the time. Despite the League's refusal to consider the Iranian protest, Tehran repeated its claim to the islands in the wake of Shaikh Sulman's approval, in the summer of 1930, of a concession to British Petroleum to explore for oil in Bahraini territory; Iran reiterated its claim three years later when the concession was taken over by Standard Oil of California. Prime Minister Ahmad Qavam as-Sultanah revived Iran's claim to the islands in 1946 by announcing that any petroleum produced in Bahrain and shipped to Anglo-Iranian facilities on the Iranian coast would be taxed at the same rate as oil produced in Iran itself; the nationalist government of Dr. Mohammad Mossadegh extended the act expropriating the operations of the Anglo-Iranian Oil Company to those of Standard Oil and its partner, the Texas Oil Company, in March 1951.[8]

Twenty years later, when Great Britain announced that its forces were withdrawing from the Gulf, Iran again claimed sovereignty over Bahrain. After repeated discussions between Iranian and British officials under the auspices of the United Nations Secretariat in the spring of 1970, Secretary-General U Thant appointed a special commissioner to ascertain whether the Bahraini population desired some form of union with Iran. Following three weeks of canvassing indigenous sentiment on this issue, the commissioner concluded that the islands' inhabitants were "virtually unanimous in wanting a fully independent sovereign state."[9] The United Nations Security Council ratified the commission's report on 11 May and the shah's regime quietly abandoned its claim to the archipelago to concentrate on retaining the strategically more important islands of Abu Musa and the Tunbs at the entrance to the Gulf.

Iranian claims to Bahrain reemerged in the wake of the Islamic revolution. During the summer of 1979, the Ayatollah Sadeq Ruhani announced that the islands constituted "the fourteenth province" of the Islamic Republic and that he intended to launch a movement to overthrow the Al Khalifah unless they adopted "an Islamic form of government similar to the one established in Iran."[10] This statement appears to have embarrassed the government of Mehdi Bazargan, which had been attempting to cultivate better relations with the Arab Gulf states. The prime minister immediately distanced himself from the Ayatollah Ruhani's remarks, calling them "unauthorized"; in late September the Iranian foreign minister, Ibrahim Yazdi, was reported to have said that the Ayatollah's views represented "only himself." By mid-October Sadeq Tabataba'i, the Islamic Republic's assistant prime minister for public relations and transition affairs, was telling regional journalists that the entire incident had been a "misunderstanding" and that Tehran had only "friendly" intentions toward Manama.

From late 1979 to the end of 1981, Iranian officials repeatedly visited Bahrain and the other Gulf amirates in an effort to ease tensions along the Islamic Republic's southern borders. Representatives arriving in Manama during this period brought messages reaffirming Tehran's desire to end the rivalry between Arabs and Persians that had characterized the policies of the Pahlavi period. At the same time, however, more militant factions within the Islamic Republic continued to broadcast calls by the Islamic Liberation Front–Bahrain and other clandestine organizations for a popular uprising against the Al Khalifah.[11] Such appeals led Bahraini police to charge that the conspirators involved in the December 1981 plot to assassinate prominent government officials on the islands had been sponsored by and trained in Iran. According to one report, an armed delegation presented the Bahraini embassy in Tehran with a note claiming responsibility for the plot at the time their comrades were arrested. This action led the foreign ministry to request that Iran recall its chargé d'affaires in Manama.[12] It also set the stage for an emergency meeting of Gulf foreign ministers in early February whose concluding communiqué pledged joint action to counter any Iranian-sponsored subversion in the region. Bahrain was reported to have favored substantially tougher measures against the Islamic Republic, including the suspension of normal economic and diplomatic relations on the part of Gulf governments. But such moves were tabled by Bahrain's allies on the grounds they might appear unduly provocative.

By mid-1982, Bahraini-Iranian relations had begun to improve. In August of that year two members of the Iranian parliament paid a "goodwill visit" to the islands as part of a tour of the Arab Gulf states. This visit was followed by a succession of economic missions to Manama over the next nine months. Plans were announced in mid-September to initiate ship-borne passenger service between Bushire–Kharq Island–Abadan and Manama–Doha–Dammam under the auspices of Islamic Republic Shipping Lines. Such contacts led the head of the political bureau of Iran's foreign ministry to visit Bahrain in May 1983 to confer with local officials regarding a variety of regional issues. These meetings resulted in the appointment of a new chargé at the Iranian embassy in Manama.

In May 1985, following the lead of Saudi Arabia's foreign minister Saud al-Faisal, Bahrain moved to put its relations with the Islamic Republic on a more normal basis. The Iranian foreign minister, Ali Akbar Velayati, dispatched a personal representative to Manama later that spring to discuss possibilities for cooperation between the two countries. This trip was followed up in October by talks between the Iranian undersecretary for foreign affairs and the Bahraini prime minister and minister of defense concerning "bilateral relations and developments in the Gulf."[13]

Iran's relations with Bahrain have thus shifted markedly during the last twenty years. In the late 1960s, Tehran demanded sovereignty over the islands on the basis of purported political ties between Bahrain and rulers on the Persian mainland. To the extent that sectarian factors were adduced at all during this period, they were considered no more than cultural vestiges of the era of Persian control over the archipelago. After the establishment of the Islamic Republic, however, the Iranian claim to the islands came to be couched in terms of the presumed right of the indigenous Shi'a to live under Shi'i authority. This claim, which struck a responsive chord among the underprivileged members of the community, largely evaporated in the wake of the aborted coup of December 1981 and subsequent developments in the war between Iran and Iraq.

RELATIONS WITH THE ARAB GULF STATES

Manama's relations with other Arab Gulf capitals in the years since independence have generally taken the form of constantly shifting alliances designed to counterbalance threats from the most dynamic of these states with close cooperative ties to the others. This dynamic has for the most part involved playing Baghdad off against Riyad, as first Iraq and then Saudi Arabia attempted to bring the islands into its sphere of influence. But it also lies at the heart of Bahraini relations with the other member-states of the Gulf Cooperation Council (GCC), in whose deliberations Manama has most often occupied a position somewhere between those members advocating complete regional self-reliance in security matters and those calling for closer collaboration with outside powers.

From 1971 to 1975 the most serious challenge to Bahraini autonomy came from Iraqi efforts to limit the influence of Western powers in the Gulf and promote social revolution throughout the region. Baghdad repeatedly criticized Manama for allowing U.S. military forces access to bases on the islands, as well as for acquiescing in what the Iraqis perceived as Iran's attempt to create a sphere of influence around the Gulf littoral. More important, the string of Iraqi trade centers opened along the southern side of the Gulf after mid-1968 served as a vehicle for spreading Ba'thi principles among local populations. The activities of these centers—along with Baghdad's decision to conclude a treaty of friendship and cooperation with the Soviet Union in April 1972—led the Bahraini regime to keep Iraq at arm's length during the early 1970s, despite the Iraqi leadership's persistent attempts to establish better relations with the other Arab Gulf states.

Under these circumstances, Bahrain cultivated closer ties with both Saudi Arabia and the other amirates as a way of counterbalancing Iraqi assertiveness. Proposals to link the islands with both the Saudi mainland and the Qatar peninsula were advanced during the first year after independence. Bahraini officials took the lead in calling for greater levels of military cooperation among the smaller Gulf states during the early 1970s, with the foreign minister proposing in November 1974 that these amirates create a regional alliance to complement the diplomatic and economic ties present in the area. Shortly after this statement, Saudi Arabia invited Shaikh 'Isa and several other rulers to observe military exercises in the kingdom; the following June the Saudi and Bahraini armed forces staged a joint exercise in which more than 1,000 troops were airlifted to designated locations in the southern part of al-Awal.

These moves accompanied efforts on the part of the regime to cultivate good relations with other Arab capitals as well. During the first week of May 1973 the amir criticized the decision taken by some Arab states to suspend economic assistance to Jordan, remarking that the Arabs were "strong in fighting each other but weak in fighting the common enemy."[14] The following year, Manama reached an agreement with Cairo whereby the two governments would share technical and engineering expertise and increase the number of educational exchanges between their respective countries.

As the Iraqi regime gradually abandoned its program of exporting Ba'thi socialism in the second half of the decade, relations between the smaller Gulf states and Baghdad started to improve. There was speculation in the aftermath of the March 1975 agreement between Iraq and Iran demarcating the boundaries of the Shatt al-Arab waterway that the two states might join Saudi Arabia in forming a mutual nonaggression pact, whose membership would later be expanded to include the amirates. Bahrain's defense minister and chief of staff visited the Iraqi capital toward the end of the year for discussions on common security concerns. These trips were followed by a series of technical and commercial missions between the two countries to promote complementary economic relations. At about the same time, a delegation of local Ba'thists journeyed to Baghdad to "explain the circumstances and dimensions of the national struggle in Bahrain" in light of shifts in Iraq's foreign affairs.[15]

In 1976–1977 the smaller Gulf states made a succession of attempts to coordinate their defense policies both with one another and with the larger states in the region. Bahrain again took the lead in advocating such cooperative arrangements, acting as a mediator between the more pro-Western regime in Oman and the avowedly nonaligned governments of Kuwait and Iraq. When it became clear that no middle ground could be found between these positions, Manama opted to negotiate a bilateral agreement with Riyad in which each party pledged to assist the other in maintaining internal security. This agreement set the pattern for subsequent pacts between Saudi Arabia, on the one hand, and Qatar, Kuwait, and the United Arab Emirates, on the other.

In early 1977 Bahrain's foreign minister reiterated his government's expectation that greater levels of interamirate cooperation would lead to the emergence of a regional consensus regarding the gradual elimination of the influence of outside powers in regional affairs. The negotiations that resulted in the termination of home-basing privileges at Jufair for the U.S. Middle East Force in July 1977 coincided with reports that Saudi Arabia was constructing a set of air and naval bases on the islands. Intraregional cooperation increased temporarily in the fall of that year when U.S. officials hinted that a U.S. naval task force might be set up to defend Western-owned oil installations in the area. This trend facilitated the sharing of information concerning dissident organizations and individuals among the intelligence services of the respective amirates, setting the stage for an Omani proposal in May 1978 that these agencies establish a joint intelligence network in the Gulf. The proposal elicited no comment from Manama but was firmly opposed by both Kuwait, which resisted any attempt to form overt alliances among the Gulf states, and Saudi Arabia, which suspected that any such regional network would be used by Tehran as a pretext for interfering in the internal affairs of its neighbors.

Increasing instability in Iran, coupled with growing Soviet involvement in the Horn of Africa and Afghanistan, pushed Bahrain into closer collaboration with the other Arab Gulf states during the course of 1978. This trend was reinforced by U.S. suggestions that its naval forces might intervene in the Gulf to protect Western interests. Bahrain, for its part, openly opposed such action: As early as mid-May Shaikh Muhammad bin Mubarak told reporters that local governments should coordinate their own defenses rather than looking to some country "miles away" to protect the area for them.[16] By the end of the year, Manama had established a particularly close working relationship with Kuwait; the next spring Shaikh Muhammad pointed to this relationship as one that could provide the nucleus for more comprehensive Gulf coordination regarding security issues. The Bahraini chief of staff commented in June 1979 that he considered the Bahrain Defense Force an extension of Kuwait's armed forces.

But concrete expression of interamirate military cooperation emerged not so much from the ties between Bahrain and Kuwait as from the links between both these states and Saudi Arabia. Bahrain's defense minister joined the rulers of Kuwait, Qatar, and the United Arab Emirates in observing large-scale maneuvers in the Saudi kingdom's southern province of Asir in late June 1979. The summit that followed these exercises initiated a series of talks among regional governments concerning the form that mutual defense might take. A Bahraini proposal to set up a combined naval task force in the Gulf failed to receive support from any of the other amirates. Consequently, when units of the Iranian navy carried out maneuvers near the islands later that fall, two brigades of Saudi infantry had to be airlifted into the country at the regime's request as a precautionary measure. This action prompted renewed negotiations between the two governments concerning the construction of a causeway connecting their respective territories.

As it appeared increasingly likely that Bahrain would be drawn into a Saudi sphere of influence, Manama moved to reestablish ties with Baghdad. This effort was facilitated by a number of important shifts in regional affairs. The overthrow of the shah's regime and the evident disorder that accompanied the Islamic revolution not only created a common threat to these two countries but also removed the possibility that Bahrain could attempt to counterbalance Saudi or Iraqi pressure by entertaining closer ties to Tehran. The Soviet intervention in Afghanistan resulted in a marked cooling of relations between Moscow and Baghdad and a consequent thaw in Iraq's relations with the Gulf states. Moreover, renewed American hints that the United States might establish a task force to protect local oil facilities led Bahraini officials to fall in with Baghdad's long-standing opposition to outside interference in regional affairs. Thus Shaikh Hamad traveled to Iraq at the start of 1980 to explore joint strategies for resisting foreign influence in the Gulf, and local companies contracted to participate in a variety of Iraqi ventures.

This process of rapprochement led Bahrain's rulers to express guarded support for Baghdad as tensions mounted between Iraq and Iran during the spring and summer of 1980. In early May, government forces suppressed a series of demonstrations by partisans of the Islamic Republic, dismissing the events as "insignificant" actions by "immature children." Immediately prior to the Iraqi attack, the Bahraini prime minister visited the Iraqi capital, telling local reporters that "Iraq's strength constitutes strength for all of us and a bulwark for our fateful course."[17] More significantly, Manama appears to have granted Iraqi commanders permission to use airfields on the islands as dispersal points in the event it became necessary to protect the country's air force from Iranian raids.

Bahraini policy toward the other Arab Gulf states thus followed a clear pattern in the decade prior to the outbreak of the Iran-Iraq war. Whenever Iraqi policy threatened to undermine Manama's stability or autonomy, the Al Khalifah cultivated closer ties with the other amirates in general and with Saudi Arabia in particular. At the same time, however, Manama attempted to balance its growing ties to Riyad by developing working relationships with Amman and a select group of other Arab capitals. As Iraq began to moderate its foreign policy in the mid-1970s, Bahrain advocated the formation of a comprehensive security arrangement involving all the Arab Gulf states. Such an institution remained the expressed goal of Bahraini security policy throughout the second half of the decade, despite the evident impracticality of the scheme and the country's increasing reliance on Saudi Arabia. The latter dynamic prompted the regime to reconsolidate its ties to Baghdad during the months just before the war in an effort to regain some degree of independence in regional affairs. In this way, the general thrust of Bahraini foreign policy contributed, albeit marginally, to create the circumstances under which Iraq launched its attack into Khuzistan in September 1980.

EFFECTS OF THE IRAN-IRAQ WAR

Iraq's failure to achieve a decisive victory over Iran in the first weeks of the Gulf war precipitated a variety of shifts in Bahraini foreign policy. In the first place, Manama attempted to distance itself from Baghdad, announcing that it occupied a neutral position between the two combatants. Second, the Bahraini government stepped up its efforts to generate support for joint diplomatic and military action among the amirates, efforts that drew the country increasingly close to neighboring Saudi Arabia. And finally, the regime began to encourage Arab states outside the Gulf to take on a more active role in defending the area.

Bahrain kept a low profile in regional diplomacy during the first winter of the war. The government protested Iranian air attacks on Kuwait in mid-November 1980 and met privately with Iraqi leaders prior to the Arab summit conference in Amman later that month. But Manama avoided sending more direct signals of support to Baghdad, falling instead behind Saudi efforts to generate coordinated security policies among the various states along the southern Gulf littoral. These efforts culminated in a conference of amirate foreign ministers in Riyad in early February 1981 at which it was agreed to set up a regional organization to provide an institutional basis for greater economic, social, and cultural cooperation among these states. The new organization—called the Cooperation Council for the States of the Arab Gulf, or Gulf Cooperation Council— was to consist of a supreme council made up of the rulers of the member-states, a ministerial council composed of their respective foreign ministers, and a secretariat charged with administering the council's affairs. It was not designed at its inception to coordinate interamirate security policy; these matters continued to be organized on a bilateral basis throughout the early months of 1981, despite urgings from Bahrain that the GCC take a more active role in providing for regional defense.

At the second meeting of the ministerial council in Taif at the beginning of September 1981, the foreign ministers of the six GCC states approved plans to cancel all customs duties on exchanges between their respective countries, to collaborate on industrial and oil policy, and to remove barriers to the movement of persons and investment funds across local boundaries. The ministers also went on record opposing any attempt by outside powers to set up military bases in the area, a declaration interpreted as criticism of the recently formed Aden Pact linking the People's Democratic Republic of Yemen, Libya, and Ethiopia. With regard to the Iran-Iraq war, the council did little more than appeal to Tehran to implement a cease-fire and reiterate its support for the attempts by the United Nations and the Islamic Conference Organization to mediate the conflict.

In the wake of the December 1981 attempt to overthrow the Al Khalifah, the GCC sharply increased its activities in the area of regional security. The Saudi interior minister visited Manama immediately after the plot was discovered and publicly accused Iran of sending agents provocateurs throughout the region. During his visit, the Bahraini and Saudi governments signed a new mutual security pact calling for greater collaboration between their respective security organizations. GCC defense ministers met in Riyad the following month to discuss the possibilities for joint action in the areas of air defense, military production and procurement, and troop deployment. By the spring of 1982, these moves had precipitated greater efforts to coordinate defense policies among the states of the lower Gulf. At a meeting of GCC chiefs of staff in mid-March, plans were drawn up for making use of the resources of the amirates' combined armed forces to improve the status of the Bahrain Defense Force. This program was no doubt intended to compensate Manama for the GCC's refusal to consider the formation of a Gulf rapid deployment force, for which Bahrain had been calling since the end of 1981.

Shaikh 'Isa convened the third meeting of the GCC supreme council in the Bahraini capital in November 1982 with praise for the organization's contributions to regional economic integration, but in the closed sessions that followed Bahraini officials were unable to persuade the rulers to reach formal agreement on cooperative measures to promote internal security and external defense. A draft agreement on domestic security was debated at this summit; it called on member-states to share information on suspected dissidents, to cooperate to stop illegal border crossings, and to consider setting up joint border patrols.[18] But measures to enhance military cooperation continued to be resisted by Kuwait on the grounds that the Arab League charter provided a sufficient basis for mutual security within the Arab world.

As Iranian forces continued to advance into Iraqi territory during 1983, and as Iranian leaders threatened to close the Strait of Hormuz if Iraq used its new French aircraft to attack oil installations at Kharq Island, GCC officials began to respond more favorably to Bahrain's calls for increased tactical coordination among the armed forces of the member-states. In August of that year, the Bahraini interior minister told reporters that progress was being made in formulating a mutual defense pact. Joint maneuvers by units of the armed forces of all the GCC states were held for the first time in mid-October as a way of ironing out logistical and technical problems preparatory to the creation of a GCC-sponsored task force. Bahrain contributed a company-sized infantry unit to these exercises. They were followed by combined maneuvers between the air defense forces of Bahrain and Qatar. With the outbreak of the so-called "tanker war" in the spring of 1984, Kuwaiti opposition to military collaboration among the GCC countries evaporated and the amirates closed ranks in open support of Baghdad, accusing Tehran of "aggression" in violation of international law and the United Nations Charter.[19] This shift in rhetoric laid the groundwork for closer cooperation between the armed forces of Saudi Arabia on the one hand and those of the other Gulf states on the other. Saudi-led regional cooperation was most apparent in the greater sharing of intelligence gathered by U.S.-operated Airborne Warning and Control System aircraft operating out of Saudi bases.

Virtually alone among the GCC states, Bahrain attempted to offset the growing influence of Saudi Arabia in Gulf security affairs by making overtures to Jordan. In the summer of 1984 the Bahraini foreign minister responded positively to Amman's offer to provide support to the Arab Gulf states in the form of equipment and troops for use in a regional rapid deployment force. This force, which had the strong backing of the United States, was rejected by almost all of the other GCC governments. But as Shaikh Muhammad told the press in early July, "We are not embarrassed to seek the help of Arab forces in defense co-operation within a national framework. We are not sensitive about it. . . . Everyone must know we are not embarrassed to seek help of Jordanian or Arab forces."[20]

INTERAMIRATE DISPUTES

Territorial disputes between Bahrain and neighboring states have been a persistent feature of interamirate relations during the years since World War II. In the wake of the Truman administration's declaration that it regarded the continental shelf around the United States to be subject to U.S. jurisdiction, boundary problems proliferated throughout the Gulf, which strictly speaking has no continental shelf at all. Bahrain responded to this state of affairs in early June 1949 by announcing that it claimed "the sea bed and the subsoil extending a reasonable distance from the shore," pending "consultation with the neighboring governments."[21] This move followed Saudi Arabia's lead in proposing that regional boundaries be drawn up through mutually satisfactory agreements by the states concerned. Nine years later, Manama and Riyad agreed to transfer the disputed area known as Fasht Abu Safah to Saudi control in exchange for annual payments of half the revenues derived from oil operations in the zone. This agreement laid the basis for a comprehensive offshore boundary treaty between these two countries.

More salient from Bahrain's perspective has been the dispute with Qatar regarding sovereignty over the Hawar archipelago. This group of 16 barren but strategically situated islands lies approximately one mile off the Qatari coast, directly between the two states. The disputed status of the group has been a continual source of tension between Manama and Doha, despite a British ruling in 1939 awarding sovereignty to Bahrain. This dispute has been credited with precluding the formation of a political union consisting of Bahrain, Qatar, and the seven Trucial States in 1971, as well as with undermining a proposed causeway linking the two countries five years later.[22]

In April 1978 Qatari leaders accused the Al Khalifah of refusing to enter serious negotiations concerning the future of the islands; they maintained that the Al Khalifah preferred instead a status quo in which the boundaries between the two countries were left undemarcated and Bahrain retained de facto jurisdiction over the territory. This charge appears to have followed maneuvers by Bahraini warships near the islands that prompted the interdiction of a number of Bahraini fishing boats by Qatari patrol vessels. The incident strained relations between Manama and Doha but was resolved through Saudi mediation. Almost exactly four years later, the Qatari government formally protested the Bahraini navy's christening one of its new frigates the *Hawar* and accused Manama of carrying out naval exercises in Qatari territorial waters.

On 26 April 1986 tension between Bahrain and Qatar flared into open conflict as Qatari troops landed on the recently reclaimed island of Fasht ad-Dibal, northeast of Muharraq. The attackers captured 29 foreign workers engaged in building a coast guard station on the island and fired at a tug lying offshore. Bahrain reacted by reinforcing its small garrison on the Hawar Islands, while Qatar put units along its western coast on alert. Omani and Saudi officials quickly traveled to Doha in an effort to mediate the conflict; this intervention led to the release of the detained workers in the second week of May. In early June, the Qatari task force began withdrawing from Fasht ad-Dibal, and the Bahrain Defense Force reciprocated by pulling its reinforcements off Hawar. By the middle of the month the crisis had ended.

CONCLUSION

Bahrain's foreign policy continues to be characterized by efforts to maintain an interrelated set of counterpoised alliances. As a way of overcoming its relatively vulnerable position in the heart of the Gulf, Manama has cultivated a tacit alliance with the predominant outside power in the region, the United States. At the same time, it has resisted successive efforts by Iran, Iraq, and Saudi Arabia to incorporate the islands into their respective spheres of influence by playing each of these regional powers off against one another. This strategy has become increasingly hard to carry out in the wake of the revolution in Iran, which deprived the regime of the option of turning to Tehran as a means of counteracting growing Saudi influence, and the outbreak of the Iran-Iraq war, which made it virtually impossible to adopt a neutral stance with regard to the two combatants.

As a result of these developments, Manama has increasingly been pulled into the orbit of Riyad when it comes to defense and security matters. This trend has been reinforced by the present structure of the Gulf Cooperation Council, which places primary responsibility for military affairs in Saudi hands. Bahrain's rulers have attempted to resist becoming subordinated to a regional defense network dominated by its larger neighbor by inviting Arab states outside the Gulf to play a more active role in promoting stability in this part of the world. Furthermore, by perpetuating boundary disputes with its GCC partners, Manama subverts the long-term viability of this pact, indirectly enhancing the country's prospects for autonomous action when peace eventually returns to the Gulf.

NOTES

1. J. E. Peterson, *Defending Arabia* (New York: St. Martin's, 1986), pp. 88–92 and 98.
2. *Arab Report and Record (ARR)*, 1–15 March 1971.
3. *ARR*, 1–15 August 1971.
4. *Middle East Journal* 29(Spring 1975), chronology entry for Persian Gulf.
5. *ARR*, 1–15 December 1974.
6. *Middle East Journal* 29(Summer 1975), chronology entry for Bahrain.
7. *ARR*, 16–30 April 1977.
8. Majid Khadduri, "Iran's Claim to the Sovereignty of Bahrayn," *American Journal of International Law* 45(October 1951), p. 631.
9. Muhammad T. Sadik and William P. Snavely, *Bahrain, Qatar, and the United Arab Emirates* (Lexington, Mass.: D. C. Heath, 1972), p. 132.
10. R. K. Ramazani, *Revolutionary Iran: Challenge and Response in the Middle East* (Baltimore: Johns Hopkins University Press, 1986), p. 49; Robert Litwak, *Security in the Persian Gulf: Sources of Inter-State Conflict* (Montclair, N.J.: Allanheld, Osmun, 1981), p. 45.
11. Litwak, *Security in the Persian Gulf*, p. 48, note 1.
12. Ramazani, *Revolutionary Iran*, pp. 50–51.

13. *Middle East Economic Digest,* 26 October 1985.

14. *ARR,* 1–15 May 1973.

15. *ARR,* 1–15 October 1975.

16. *ARR,* 1–15 May 1978.

17. Gerd Nonneman, *Iraq, the Gulf States and the War* (London: Ithaca Press, 1986), p. 21.

18. *Middle East Contemporary Survey 1982–1983,* pp. 451–452.

19. *Middle East Contemporary Survey 1983–1984,* p. 393.

20. Ibid., p. 400.

21. A translation of the proclamation appears in *American Journal of International Law* 43(Supplement 1949), pp. 185–186.

22. Litwak, *Security in the Persian Gulf,* p. 49; *ARR,* 1–15 April 1976.

Suggestions for Further Reading

General introductions to Bahrain may be found in James H. D. Belgrave, *Welcome to Bahrain* (Manama: privately published, 1960); Angela Clarke, *The Islands of Bahrain: An Illustrated Guide to Their Heritage* (Manama: Bahrain Historical and Archaeological Society, 1981); Michael Jenner, *Bahrain: Gulf Heritage in Transition* (London: Longman, 1985); John Bulloch, *The Persian Gulf Unveiled* (New York: Congdon and Weed, 1984); and Molly Izzard, *The Gulf: Arabia's Western Approaches* (London: John Murray, 1979).

CHAPTER 1: GEOGRAPHICAL AND SOCIAL STRUCTURE

Two studies are essential for an understanding of Bahrain's social geography: Fuad I. Khuri, *Tribe and State in Bahrain* (Chicago: University of Chicago Press, 1980) and Mohammed Ghanim al-Rumaihi, *Bahrain: A Study on Social and Political Changes Since the First World War* (Kuwait: University of Kuwait Press, 1975). Further information on the islands' topography may be found in Curtis E. Larsen, *Life and Land Use on the Bahrain Islands* (Chicago: University of Chicago Press, 1983). Village society is discussed by Henny Harald Hansen, *Investigations in a Shi'a Village in Bahrain* (Copenhagen: National Museum of Denmark, 1968) and in "The Pattern of Women's Seclusion and Veiling in a Shi'a Village," *Folk* 3(1961); R. B. Serjeant, "Fisher-folk and Fish-traps in al-Bahrain," *Bulletin of the School of Oriental and African Studies* 31(1968); and, for earlier periods, Sheila A. Scoville, ed., *Gazetter of Arabia: A Geographical and Tribal History of the Arabian Peninsula* (Graz: Akademische Druck- und Verlagsanstalt, 1979). Also enlightening is Clive D. Holes, "Patterns of Communal Language Variation in Bahrain," *Language in Society* 12(December 1983), which covers considerably more ground than its title indicates.

On issues of urbanization, past and present, see Michael E. Bonine, "The Urbanization of the Persian Gulf Nations," in Alvin J. Cottrell, ed., *The Persian Gulf States: A General Survey* (Baltimore: Johns Hopkins University Press, 1980); N. C. Grill, *Urbanisation in the Arabian Peninsula*, Centre for Middle Eastern and Islamic Studies, University of Durham, Occasional Papers Series, No. 25(1984); Allan G. Hill, "Population, Migration and Development in the Gulf States," in Shahram Chubin, ed., *Security in the Persian Gulf: Domestic Political Factors* (Montclair, N.J.: Allanheld, Osmun, 1981); Geoffrey King, "Bayt Al-Mu'ayyad: A Late Nineteenth-Century House of al-Bahrayn," in R. B. Serjeant and R. L. Bidwell, eds., *Arabian Studies*, volume 4 (London: C. Hurst, 1978); and John Dyckman, Alan Kreditor, and Tridib Banerjee, "Planning in an Unprepared Environment: The Example of Bahrain," *Town Planning Review* 55(April 1984).

Other aspects of societal change are dealt with in Ralph H. Magnus, "Societies and Social Change in the Persian Gulf," and Michael M. J. Fischer, "Competing Ideologies and Social Structure in the Persian Gulf," both in Cottrell, *The Persian Gulf States*; Shirley B. Taylor, "Some Aspects of Social Change and Modernization in Bahrain," in Jeffrey B. Nugent and Theodore H. Thomas, eds., *Bahrain and the Gulf* (New York: St. Martin's, 1985); Rob Franklin, "Migrant Labor and the Politics of Development in Bahrain," *MERIP Reports* 132(May 1985); and, in a very different fashion, Abdulrahman Obaid Musaiger, "The Impact of Television Food Advertisements on Dietary Behaviour of Bahraini Housewives," *Ecology of Food and Nutrition* 13(April 1983). Immigrant workers are covered by J. S. Birks and C. A. Sinclair, *Arab Manpower* (New York: St. Martin's, 1980).

Women's roles are analyzed in Nesta Ramazani, "The Veil—Piety or Protest?" *Journal of South Asian and Middle Eastern Studies* 7(Winter 1983); E. James Fordyce, Layla Rhadi, Maurice D. Van Arsdol, Jr., and Mary Beard Deming, "The Changing Roles of Arab Women in Bahrain," in Nugent and Thomas, *Bahrain and the Gulf*; and, from a somewhat contradictory viewpoint, in Fadwa El Guindi, "The Status of Women in Bahrain: Social and Cultural Considerations," in the same volume.

CHAPTER 2: THE ESTABLISHMENT OF THE BRITISH IMPERIAL ORDER

Bahrain's ancient history is surveyed by Geoffrey Bibby, *Looking for Dilmun* (New York: Knopf, 1969), and Michael Rice, *Search for the Paradise Land* (London: Longman, 1985). A set of stimulating essays may be found in Shaikha Haya Ali Al Khalifa and Michael Rice, eds., *Bahrain Through the Ages: The Archaeology* (London: KPI, 1986), of which Christopher Edens, "Bahrain and the Arabian Gulf During the Second Millennium B.C.: Urban Crisis and Colonialism," and Gerd Weisgerber, "Dilmun—A Trading Entrepot: Evidence from Historical and Archaeological Sources," stand out. In the same collection, G. W. Bowersock, "Tylos and Tyre: Bahrain in the Graeco-Roman World," deals with the subsequent era. The transition to the Islamic period is treated in Richard N. Frye, "Bahrain Under the Sasanians," in Daniel T. Potts, ed., *Dilmun: New Studies in the Archaeology and Early History of Bahrain* (Berlin: Dietrich Reimer Verlag, 1983); Roger M. Savory, "A.D. 600–1800," in Cottrell, *The Persian Gulf States*; Elias S. Shoufani, *Al-Riddah and the Muslim Conquest of Arabia* (Toronto: University of Toronto Press, 1973); and Hugh Kennedy, "The Desert and the Sown in Eastern

Arabian History," in Ian Richard Netton, ed., *Arabia and the Gulf: From Traditional Society to Modern States* (Totowa, N.J.: Barnes and Noble, 1986).

Medieval times are outlined in Andrew Williamson, "Hurmuz and the Trade of the Gulf in the 14th and 15th Centuries A.D.," in the Proceedings of the Sixth Seminar for Arabian Studies, Institute of Archaeology, London, September 1972; Juan R. I. Cole, "Rival Empires of Trade and Imami Shi'ism in Eastern Arabia, 1300–1800," *International Journal of Middle East Studies* 19(May 1987); and Salih Ozbaran, "The Ottoman Turks and the Portuguese in the Persian Gulf, 1534–1581," *Journal of Asian History* 6(1972).

For the modern period, Ahmad Abu Hakima, *History of Eastern Arabia: The Rise and Development of Bahrain and Kuwait* (Beirut: Khayats, 1965) is essential; see also his article "The Development of the Gulf States," in Derek Hopwood, ed., *The Arabian Peninsula: Society and Politics* (Totowa, N.J.: Rowman and Littlefield, 1972). On the structure of tribal rule before the coming of the British, see Peter Lienhardt, "The Authority of Shaykhs in the Gulf: An Essay in Nineteenth-Century History," in R. B. Serjeant and R. L. Bidwell, eds., *Arabian Studies*, volume 2 (London: C. Hurst, 1975), and J. E. Peterson, "Tribes and Politics in Eastern Arabia," *Middle East Journal* 31(Summer 1977).

Pearling in Bahrain is the subject of Mohamed G. Rumaihi, "The Mode of Production in the Arab Gulf Before the Discovery of Oil," in Tim Niblock, ed., *Social and Economic Development in the Arab Gulf* (New York: St. Martin's, 1980); Samar K. Datta and Jeffrey B. Nugent, "Bahrain's Pearling Industry: How It Was, Why It Was That Way and Its Implications," in Nugent and Thomas, *Bahrain and the Gulf*; and George Rentz, "Pearling in the Persian Gulf," in Walter J. Fischel, ed., *Semitic and Oriental Studies* (Berkeley: University of California Press, 1951).

Britain's entry into the Gulf is cogently summarized in Abdul Amir Amin, *British Interests in the Persian Gulf* (Leiden: E. J. Brill, 1967). Subsequent developments may be found in J. B. Kelly's magisterial study *Britain and the Persian Gulf 1795–1880* (Oxford: Oxford University Press, 1968), as well as in J. F. Standish, "British Maritime Policy in the Persian Gulf," *Middle Eastern Studies* 3(July 1967); two essays by Malcolm Yapp, "The Nineteenth and Twentieth Centuries" and "British Policy in the Persian Gulf," both in Cottrell, *The Persian Gulf States;* and Arnold T. Wilson, *The Persian Gulf* (London: Allen and Unwin, 1928). Whether the Arab states in fact practiced piracy at the beginning of the nineteenth century is questioned by Sultan Muhammad Al-Qasimi, *The Myth of Arab Piracy in the Gulf* (London: Croom Helm, 1986), and Patricia R. Dubuisson, "Qasimi Piracy and the General Treaty of Peace (1820)," in R. B. Serjeant and R. L. Bidwell, eds., *Arabian Studies*, volume 4 (London: C. Hurst, 1978).

Late-nineteenth-century trends are ably surveyed in Talal Toufic Farah, *Protection and Politics in Bahrain 1869–1915* (Beirut: American University of Beirut Press, 1985), and Briton Cooper Busch, *Britain and the Persian Gulf, 1894–1914* (Berkeley: University of California Press, 1967). These overviews may be supplemented by looking at Lovat Fraser, "Gun-running in the Persian Gulf," *Proceedings of the Central Asia Society* (London, May 1911), and Stephanie Jones, "The Management of British India Steamers in the Gulf 1862–1945," in R. I.

Lawless, ed., *The Gulf in the Early 20th. Century,* Centre for Middle Eastern and Islamic Studies, University of Durham, Occasional Papers Series, No. 31(1986). Initial aircraft and petroleum concessions are the subject of G. W. Bentley, "The Development of the Air Route in the Persian Gulf," *Journal of the Royal Central Asian Society* 20(April 1933), and Rosemarie Said Zahlan, "The Impact of the Early Oil Concessions in the Gulf States," in Lawless, *The Gulf in the Early 20th. Century.* How these trends came out may be gleaned from Penelope Tuson, *The Records of the British Residency and Agencies in the Persian Gulf* (London: India Office Records, 1979), and R. M. Burrell, "Britain, Iran and the Persian Gulf: Some Aspects of the Situation in the 1920s and 1930s," in Hopwood, *The Arabian Peninsula.* Amin Rihani, *Around the Coasts of Arabia* (London: Constable, 1930), provides a glimpse of local conditions soon after the turn of the century.

CHAPTER 3: THE NATIONALIST MOVEMENTS OF THE 1950s

Bahrain's earlier reform movement of 1938, which some argue set the precedent for the events of the mid-1950s, is described in al-Rumaihi, *Bahrain,* Part 4, Chapter 2; Rosemarie Said Zahlan characterizes a parallel movement in her "The 1938 Reform Movement in Dubai," *al-Abhath* (Beirut) 23(December 1970). Both of these authors will be dissatisfied that I have not covered the events of 1938 in this study. The war years are the subject of Robin Bidwell, "Bahrain in the Second World War," *Dilmun* 12(1984/85).

Labor affairs may be approached through Ian J. Seccombe's path-breaking "Labour Migration to the Arabian Gulf: Evolution and Characteristics 1920–1950," *Bulletin of the British Society for Middle East Studies* 10(1983); Rupert Hay, "The Impact of the Oil Industry on the Persian Gulf Shaykhdoms," *Middle East Journal* 9(Autumn 1955); David Finnie, "Recruitment and Training of Labour: The Middle East Oil Industry," *Middle East Journal* 12(Spring 1958); and Willard A. Beling, "Recent Developments in Labor Relations in Bahrayn," *Middle East Journal* 13(Spring 1959).

The best accounts of the liberal nationalist movement itself are to be found in Khuri, *Tribe and State,* and al-Rumaihi, *Bahrain;* but one should not overlook the memoirs of the British adviser on the islands, Charles Belgrave, *Personal Column* (London: Hutchinson, 1960). Also enlightening is Fahim I. Qubain, "Social Classes and Tensions in Bahrain," *Middle East Journal* 9(Summer 1955).

CHAPTER 4: CONTEMPORARY POLITICS

For standard accounts of the country's political structure, see John Duke Anthony, *Arab States of the Lower Gulf: People, Politics, Petroleum* (Washington, D.C.: Middle East Institute, 1975); Emile A. Nakhleh, *Bahrain* (Lexington, Mass.: D. C. Heath, 1976); and Muhammad T. Sadik and William P. Snavely, *Bahrain, Qatar, and the United Arab Emirates* (Lexington, Mass.: D. C. Heath, 1972). This perspective is summarized in Arnold Hottinger, "Political Institutions in Saudi Arabia, Kuwait and Bahrain," in Chubin, *Security in the Persian Gulf.* Somewhat less institutional accounts may be found in Michael Field, *The Merchants: The*

Big Business Families of Saudi Arabia and the Gulf States (Woodstock, N.Y.: Overlook Press, 1985), and Frank Stoakes, "Social and Political Change in the Third World: Some Peculiarities of Oil-Producing Principalities of the Persian Gulf," in Hopwood, *The Arabian Peninsula.*

For critical perspectives on the current regime, see Fred Halliday, *Arabia Without Sultans* (Harmondsworth: Penguin, 1974); 'Abd ul-Hadi Khalaf, "Labor Movements in Bahrain," *MERIP Reports* 132(May 1985); and, from a completely different point of view, Abdul Kasim Mansur, "The Military Balance in the Persian Gulf: Who Will Guard the Gulf States from Their Guardians?" *Armed Forces Journal International* 118(November 1980).

Parliamentary politics are dissected in Nakhleh, *Bahrain,* as well as in his comparative essay "Political Participation and the Constitutional Experiments in the Arab Gulf: Bahrain and Qatar," in Niblock, *Social and Economic Development in the Arab Gulf.*

CHAPTER 5: CONTEMPORARY ECONOMIC AFFAIRS

Economic trends may best be followed in the pages of the *Middle East Economic Digest* (London). Of the few general surveys of the Bahraini economy, the most useful are Michael Field, "Economic Problems of Arabian Peninsula Oil States," in Chubin, *Security in the Persian Gulf;* J. S. Birks and C. A. Sinclair, "Preparations for Income After Oil: Bahrain's Example," *Bulletin of the British Society for Middle East Studies* 6(1979); and Denys Brunsden, "Bahraini Strategy for Prosperity," *Geographical Magazine* 52(February 1980).

Petroleum matters provide the focus of George Lenczowski, *Oil and State in the Middle East* (Ithaca: Cornell University Press, 1960), and Keith McLachlan, "Oil in the Persian Gulf Area," in Cottrell, *The Persian Gulf States.* The financial sector is analyzed in A. S. Gerakis and O. Roncesvalles, "Bahrain's Offshore Banking Center," *Economic Development and Cultural Change* 31(January 1983); Elias T. Ghantus, "The Financial Center and Its Future," in Nugent and Thomas, *Bahrain and the Gulf;* and Rodney Wilson, *Banking and Finance in the Arab Middle East* (New York: St. Martin's, 1983).

CHAPTER 6: FOREIGN RELATIONS

Britain's withdrawal from the Gulf is the subject of D. C. Watt, "Britain and the Future of the Persian Gulf States," *World Today* 20(November 1964) and his "The Decision to Withdraw from the Gulf," *Political Quarterly* 39(July-September 1968); *The Gulf: Implications of British Withdrawal* (Washington, D.C.: Georgetown University Center for Strategic and International Studies, February 1969); David Holden, "The Persian Gulf: After the British Raj," *Foreign Affairs* 49(July 1971); and J. B. Kelly, *Arabia, the Gulf and the West: A Critical View of the Arabs and Their Oil Policy* (New York: Basic Books, 1980).

The transition from British to U.S. hegemony in the region has yet to be studied in detail. Provocative first cuts may be found in Rosemarie Said Zahlan, "Anglo-American Rivalry in Bahrain 1918–1947," *Dilmun* 12(1984/85), and J. E.

Peterson, *Defending Arabia* (London: Croom Helm, 1986). For the U.S. Raj, consult Anthony H. Cordesman, *The Gulf and the Search for Strategic Stability* (Boulder, Colo.: Westview Press, 1984), and Mazher A. Hameed, *Arabia Imperilled: The Security Imperatives of the Arab Gulf States* (Washington, D.C.: Middle East Assessments Group, 1986).

On Iran's claims to the islands, consult Fereydoun Adamiyat, *Bahrein Islands: A Legal and Diplomatic Study of the British-Iranian Controversy* (New York: Praeger, 1955); Majid Khadduri, "Iran's Claim to the Sovereignty of Bahrayn," *American Journal of International Law* 45(October 1951); and J. B. Kelly, "The Persian Claim to Bahrein," *International Affairs* 33(January 1957). Later relations between Tehran and Manama are discussed in Amir Teheri, "Policies of Iran in the Persian Gulf Region," in Abbas Amirie, ed., *The Persian Gulf and Indian Ocean in International Politics* (Tehran: Institute for International Political and Economic Studies, 1975); R. K. Ramazani, "Iran's Islamic Revolution and the Persian Gulf," *Current History* 84(January 1985), and his *Revolutionary Iran: Challenge and Response in the Middle East* (Baltimore: Johns Hopkins University Press, 1986); and Gary Sick, "Iran's Quest for Superpower Status," *Foreign Affairs* 65(Spring 1987).

John Duke Anthony's article "The Union of Arab Amirates," *Middle East Journal* 26(Summer 1972) remains the clearest survey of relations among the smaller Gulf states. But deserving of mention is R. M. Burrell, "Policies of the Arab Littoral States in the Persian Gulf Region," in Amirie, *The Persian Gulf and Indian Ocean.*

Consequences of the war between Iran and Iraq are discussed in Jonathan Farley, "The Gulf War and the Littoral States," *World Today* 40(July 1984); Gerd Nonneman, *Iraq, the Gulf States and the War* (London: Ithaca Press, 1986); and the relevant sections of Ramazani, *Revolutionary Iran.*

Territorial and other disputes among the Gulf amirates are listed in Husain M. Al-Baharna, *The Legal Status of the Arabian Gulf States* (Manchester: Manchester University Press, 1968); Robert Litwak, *Security in the Persian Gulf: Sources of Inter-State Conflict* (Montclair, N.J.: Allanheld, Osmun, 1981); Rupert Hay, "The Persian Gulf States and Their Boundary Problems," *Geographical Journal* 120(December 1954); and Will D. Swearingen, "Sources of Conflict over Oil in the Persian/Arabian Gulf," *Middle East Journal* 35(Summer 1981). For a more hopeful look into the future, see Muhammad Rumaihi, *Beyond Oil: Unity and Development in the Gulf* (London: Al Saqi Books, 1986).

Index

143